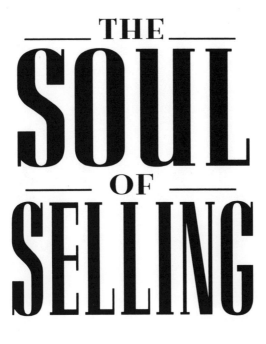

THE
SOUL
OF
SELLING

THE
SOUL
OF
SELLING

How to Focus Your Energy To
Achieve a Successful And
Happy Sales Career

Billy L. Skinner

amacom
American Management Association

New York • Atlanta • Boston • Chicago • Kansas City • San Francisco • Washington, D.C.
Brussels • Mexico City • Tokyo • Toronto

This book is available at a special
discount when ordered in bulk quantities.
For information, contact Special Sales Department,
AMACOM, a division of American Management Association,
135 West 50th Street, New York, NY 10020.

This publication is designed to provide accurate and authoritative information in regard to the subject matter covered. It is sold with the
understanding that the publisher is not engaged in rendering legal,
accounting, or other professional service. If legal advice or other expert assistance is required, the services of a competent professional
person should be sought.

Library of Congress Cataloging-in-Publication Data

Skinner, Billy L.
   The soul of selling : how to focus your energy to achieve a
successful and happy sales career / Billy L. Skinner.
      p.   cm.
   ISBN 0-8144-7874-3
   1. Selling.   I. Title.
HF5438.25.S6   1995
658.85—dc20   94-27598
                                                           CIP

Printing number

10   9   8   7   6   5   4   3   2   1

Dedicated to **Emmitt Skinner,** whose insights into the human drama were both beautiful and bountiful, and **Charlie Miller,** a sales manager whose character and conviction gave special meaning to the concept of "role model."

Contents

It is my privilege to speak for a large number of sales conferences. One of the extra benefits is that when I do so, I usually get to hear other speakers. Generally, they are of the highest quality. They are artists. They have honed their art of delivering motivational addresses so that what they have to say is not only intelligent, but entertaining. However, these motivational talks often raise ethical questions.

Not too long ago, I was at a sales conference for a major insurance corporation, and I had arrived early enough to take in the message of the speaker that preceded me on the program. The man was humorous and articulate. His delivery marked him as one of the very best speakers in the field. But what he had to say not only surprised me but also made me angry.

The content of his message was, "How to Sell an Insurance Policy to Someone Who Doesn't Need It." The presentation was a masterpiece. The man carefully identified which "emotional buttons" to push in making such a presentation. He explained to his audience how to play on people's fears and anxieties so that they will put their name on the dotted line of the contract for a product that was *not* needed.

Contrast that with the àctual situation of a man named Martin England. He is the man who sold the insurance policy to Martin Luther King. When he found out that King was uninsured, he sought him out, convinced him of his responsibility to care for the needs of his family, and made him see that buying the insurance policy would be one of the best things that he could do. King bought the policy; it was not long after that he was killed by an assassin's bullet.

After the funeral, Corretta King and her family had little in the way of money, because Martin Luther King was not a rich man. However, the insurance policy that was sold to him by Martin England provided for the family in the desperate days that followed. The children went to college, and Corretta King led a life of relative comfort: all because the salesman saw a need and met it.

I tell you these two stories to set up a contrast. In a sales technique that treats a human being as a "thing" to be manipulated, the client is an "it" to be used for no other purpose than to enhance the well-being of the salesperson. Martin England, on the other hand, sees his client as a human being and treats him as such. While Martin England made a profit on his sale, he did not make that profit at the price of his own humanity, or by diminishing the dignity of the person he was serving.

People are not to be treated like Pavlovian dogs. We are not to set them up to respond to the proper stimuli. People's needs and feelings are sacred, and the best kind of salesperson recognizes that.

In this book, Bill Skinner, a skilled salesperson and a leader in his field, tells us what he has learned about the art of sales. He shows that it is possible to do good and to do well at the same time. While not neglecting a desire to make a profit, he demonstrates the great profit to be made by understanding the needs of clients, and by using that understanding to further marketing purposes. At the end of a good sale, the salesperson is richer materially, mentally, and emotionally. And the client feels that he or she has gotten a great deal. Sales should always be a "win-win" arrangement, and Bill Skinner shows us how to make it just that.

I have found Mr. Skinner to be atypical of what I usually run into when I meet sales managers and directors of major corporations. He is not simply a "hail-fellow-well-met." There is nothing of Willy Loman's attitude about him. He is not a character out of an Arthur Miller play. Instead, he talks about human things, particularly the values related to his commitment to caring for people. He talks about the bottom line in any sales transaction that is not simply the driving need of the salesperson, but also the well being of a client. I am impressed with his sensitivity and understanding of personal interaction as related to sales, and I think that you will be impressed by this book.

—*Tony Campolo, Ph.D.*
Professor of Sociology
Eastern College
St. Davids, Pa.

I hope your reaction to this book is, "I can approach selling from the perspective of where I am and who I am." If so, I will have accomplished my mission: to convince you that you have the emotional and mental energy to create a happy, successful sales personality from within yourself, from "where you are and who you are." My major premise is clear and concise: the marvelous art of selling wells up from deep within the human personality.

Unlike pundits who have attempted to reduce, transform, and reformat the basic common-sense principles of selling into a series of trivial, often meaningless recipes, I believe selling is primarily a matter of living life to its fullest. Selling is not putting on facades. Its clearest manifestation is sincere concern for the wants and needs of fellow human beings in a spirit that calls for giving more than you get. Selling creates genuine value. Good reader, if you are fortunate enough to have chosen selling as your career, you have chosen one way to live life to its fullest 365 days a year. You have chosen a career that offers a high quality of life, tapping into your physical, emotional, mental, and even spiritual life.

I believe one's invitation to this way of life begins with a very definite, conscious wake-up call, whereby the person becomes aware that being true to one's self is the key to a happy, successful career. With this wake-up call comes the awareness that you must be yourself always and everywhere, and the resolve to share that self with others. This means putting a priority on knowing your strengths and shoring up your weaknesses, since you cannot share what you do not possess. What you possess from this perspective means, really, that of which you have personal ownership. You believe in it--you believe as though you created it. You *possess* it!

From this awareness comes a deep sense of self-esteem and self-worth that enhances appreciation of others. These awareness stages are critical, since the selling interaction is a sharing of who you are and what you have with another who accepts the same.

Selling transforms controlled human interaction and communication into trades that pay off for everyone involved. Everyone wins! Selling is that positive manipulation that has its roots in relationship intimacy. Selling seeks its own way, but the customer is the greater beneficiary. Selling is the irony of getting what you desire with the side effect of enhancing the *customer's* quality of life. If this book leaves you with an awareness that caring what happens to others is the greatest selling skill, it will have done its work and you will be ready to embrace the soul of selling.

—*Billy L. Skinner*

Thanks to Cathy McManus, who typed the manuscripts from dictated tapes and other materials, and Tom Gallagher, whose input and creativity afforded the material a reasonable flow and symmetry.

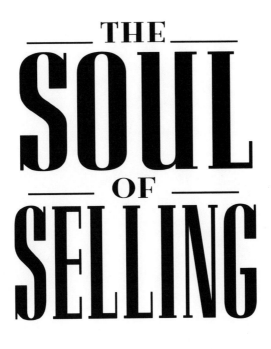

THE SOUL OF SELLING

1. The Wake-Up Call

Our sales(persons) are heroes because they're the ones we expect to interpret the customer's needs. Nothing happens until somebody sells something . . . they're at risk. They have the ability to lose. Number one, to be a hero . . .

F. G. "Buck" Rodgers

He was a salesman! Sometimes he sold his products in the poorest section of town but made certain his customers got a good buy. Always he talked to them about what was going on in their lives. To pay for college, he sold books in the summer to people in rural America's poorest sections. He made certain that the books he sold enhanced the quality of life of those who purchased. He sold new ideas to returning war veterans about how to conduct their new lives, both in business and on a personal basis. He sold his children on the idea that true freedom is a fierce independence that pre-

1

serves doing one's own thinking and establishing life values. He "gave" his influence and wisdom to the community and his family. He was an impact player . . . he made the difference with so many, many people. He was a role model; he was a "sales" hero! He was a farmer . . . .

The importance of the competent, responsible salesperson to the success of the organization is incontrovertible. I subscribe fully to the concept of the salesperson as hero. In fact, numbered among good friends are many who fill the bill as genuine heroes — a hero being one who commands from others the desire to be like himself or herself. One who has impact. One who leads the way. One who makes things happen. One who inspires others to dream. A few of them are what you could call natural-born salespeople. Surprisingly, the majority are not. But natural or not, all truly great salespeople are bona fide heroes. Rightly so — because others want to be like them, they have high impact. They make things happen and they inspire.

In a free enterprise society, salespeople are among the most prominent role models, except for sports and entertainment figures. While salespeople have widely diverse personalities and backgrounds, the hallmark of the true salesperson is self-awareness, a very real sense of self. This is more than the rational, "I think, therefore I am." To a person, these successful people are confident of who they are and where they are going. They know generally the kind of people they are. They know how they want to be perceived and how, in fact, they are perceived by others. They know that, by profession, they invite others to view them much as they view themselves. It may be a form of masochism, but they really do want to know how they look under the light. As a result, they are highly aware of and are very sensitive to their own vulnerability. But they are just as sure that, within the framework of the selling dialogue, the risks are worth it, because phonies and phony personalities just don't "cut it" in professional sales.

Hence, a plea to the would-be successful salesperson: Be yourself. It's essential since your personality is the living personal element that animates your every thought, word, and action.

If you have problems with this search for the real you, make plans to stage a self-awakening: set your mental alarm for a wake-up call. Get in tune with yourself. Start a reality-based self-analysis. What are my *real* strengths? How much do I really enjoy and accept other people — particularly people different from me? What are some tendencies that I exhibit springing from my particular personality? What kind of person am I, really? Does how I want to be perceived differ from how I really am perceived? Seriously, who is this inner person that is *me*?

Without this desire to work from within your own personality, all the training and sales techniques in the world are a waste of time. As you will see in the pages that follow, much of what this text has to offer focuses on the personal human dynamic of the sales interaction.

Make no mistake about it: selling is a difficult career. As rewarding and self-satisfying as a sales career can be when carried out well, it can be a real nightmare for anyone who does not respect or recognize the natural self-discipline required for sales success. More on this later. Pity the poor recent graduate or the person looking to escape a desk-bound, task-oriented job who, lured by the sirens of freedom, brings a "Disney World" attitude to a sales position. Typically, the naive or uninformed envision the salesperson as another well-dressed free spirit who drives around in a late-model car, expounding to whomever. And, naturally, recording the sales in an American Express organizer book. Reality, of course, makes quick work of this erroneous, simplistic impression. Still, some never recover from the career-ending shock. Fortunately, a good number of new sales candidates are highly motivated, hardworking people. Even these individuals, new-found enthusiasm notwithstanding, are awed by the responsibility that comes with the sales territory. Often, their entry into sales is the first time they alone are truly in control of their own destinies. How they accept this challenge with all its inherent responsibility will determine their long-term success and happiness.

Taking Control

A word on the natural self-discipline required to ensure this success. First, it's discipline that comes from believing that each of us has a responsibility to give something in return for the gifts we have received. It's a debt we truly owe: to pay back for something that's been given to us. This natural self-discipline is a must for the salesperson: give-back for taking. It's being responsible.

Second, it entails a high degree of caring for other people. Again, this requires discipline, because it's easy to feel that everything should come our way. We are tempted to take rather than give. To give requires self-discipline. It means a conscious desire to care and share. Then do it! On the personal level, it's the same discipline that prompts doing those "I-love-you" kinds of things so meaningful to one's beloved.

Third, the salesperson must possess self-discipline that springs from courage: courage to show one's vulnerability and the social courage to seek out reality in others. Building on one's natural courage, the salesperson must still practice facing reality in any number of scenarios aimed at discovering the customer's real needs. This "social courage," a term coined by noted psychiatrist and author Rollo May, requires that the salesperson become involved with another person at a depth level.

"It is the courage to relate to other human beings, the capacity to risk one's self in the hope of achieving meaningful intimacy. It is the courage to invest one's self over a period of time in a relationship that will demand increasing openness," says May.

The good news is that taking control of one's professional life is achievable. Scott Peck, the psychiatrist and author, suggests that all the tools needed to acquire discipline, including acceptance of responsibility, are well known to us by the time we are ten years old. Given the truth of this, most of us still spend a long time "a growin'."

It's important to understand that stereotypical self-discipline, in an extreme sense, is not predictably an asset to the salesperson. A self-discipline that prompts extreme activities, such as programming every minute of every day by rigorous timetables, believing in absolutes that suit virtually all occasions, exacting every calorie, and trimming every ounce of fat off, can be self-defeating. You know the type. Such radical disciplinarians also tend to measure out the amount of care and love given to other people. They are quick to judge people who do not share their narrow focus. Their self-centeredness makes them poor candidates for career selling.

It's important to distinguish between this concept of discipline and the natural self-discipline of responsibility, care, and courage. Literal, *extreme* self-discipline is almost always a character flaw. It produces bores and prudes as well as egocentrics who really don't care much about other people. The discipline of responsibility, care, and courage of which we speak is "other-oriented." This is the kind of discipline that makes for good sales interaction.

The Salesperson

Another pejorative stereotype of the salesperson views the professional representative as a not-so-subtle barker who peddles the real or imagined values of his wares to the buyer-victim. Willy Loman doing it all with "a smile and a shoeshine" in *Death of a Salesman* is alive and well in many minds. And that's good, because art imitates life. What most people forget, however, is that Willy was a failure as a human being long before he failed as a salesman. The play is recommended reading for all who aspire to sales, because it demonstrates clearly that Willy, despite his manic enthusiasm, failed because he assumed a phony personality that caused him to self-destruct. He cared little for his customers' real needs or how the products he sold met those needs. His credo was *caveat emptor!* The man never *really* understood.

Who is today's Willy Loman? This contemporary Willy is a direct opposite of the old version and, oddly enough, is often encouraged by marketing or sales managements that tend to *over*emphasize the information and "things" content of the sales dialogue.

Don't misunderstand me here. Sound product knowledge is a moral imperative for every professional salesperson. My quarrel is with the view that the salesperson is some kind of oracle whose main function is simply to relay rehearsed information to an eagerly awaiting, information-starved customer. This is particularly true in industries where the volume or complexity of the product knowledge, as well as its importance, could lead to the belief that the salesperson's primary mission is only one of "information transfer." Malignant notion! To anyone who thinks this way, I say: the myriad of customers is not out there waiting just for the latest golden nuggets of information on products. They are really waiting for the scenario that results in feeling better about themselves. **Even wonder products must be sold!**

Those who lead the pack in sales will be the sensitive salespersons, always searching for the *real* problems, always pressing to assure that the scenario produces good. To give the action "realized value" for the players is the real game. The salesperson as glorified interactive computer or tape recorder won't work. It's a terrible misuse of people power, and a terrible misunderstanding of human nature. Such a view can spell sales (and people) disaster.

Who, then, is the truly professional salesperson? In any industry, this person can be defined by function: the salesperson motivates another person to act on his or her behalf for the customer's benefit and profit for the salesperson's company. The other person (buyer) may not have planned this action prior to the interaction with the salesperson.

Note that there are two people involved in this equation, the salesperson and the customer. Presumably, the customer has been selected on the basis of need and the ability of the salesperson's product to fill all or part of that need. It certainly seems simple enough. This type of human interaction takes place millions of times a day from the fishermen's wharf to the White House — wherever people are trying to sell their products or ideas.

We're actually all salespeople to some degree, no matter what we do to earn our daily bread. At many junctures of our lives, we must sell others on our ideas or inclinations. That's true. But the professional salesperson dedicates her or his professional career to motivating others systematically in order to get her or his way. It sounds selfish, I know, but it isn't. Motivating others to act on your behalf within the professional selling scenario is a positive manipulation, and it's what makes selling the supremely challenging endeavor it is. It is this positive manipulation that causes something of benefit to happen to both parties — something that would otherwise not have occurred. The professional salesperson commits to making something tangible happen on every single call. Never do something tangible in a vacuum, notes the pro!

The Inner Fire

Notice that nowhere in this description of sales have we yet focused on the information content of the sales message. Of course, the sales presentation must contain relevant facts, features, advantages, and benefits, but if you say only these good things in a monotone or if you fail to personalize the sales call, you may be sure that very little or nothing positive can or will happen.

We've seen that it's not enough to want the trappings of freedom offered by sales, and that it is not enough to have the intelligence to understand and work with complex product knowledge or scientific concepts. The question to ask yourself is: Do I have the deep-down-inside-me desire to spend my working career attempting to motivate people to do what I want them to do on every sales call I make? Am I that type of person? Do I feel comfortable enough with people to feel confident that I can sway them to act on my behalf, simply on the basis of my asking them? Do I care about people to the extent that I would actually crusade to fulfill their needs? Do I even get involved in conflict to fulfill their needs? Do I have it in me? Will doing this every day fulfill me as a person — make me happy?

These are not random questions, nor do they exhaust all the questions in this self-examination. Each represents a critical issue. You would be amazed at the number of dispirited, unhappy persons who go through an entire sales career without proper consideration of the basic issues. Sure, they know they're unhappy but they make circumstances or the company's lack of support the scapegoat for their personal failures. Better for them to have heeded the view of Socrates, "The unexamined life is not worth living." That is what we are about here. The decision to enter sales or stay in sales is one of critical choice and should be made by the person after reality-based consideration of all its aspects.

This inner colloquy is an integral part of the wake-up call for success in selling. How do we initiate this awakening, this illumination of the core of one's being? Actually, the first words of the wake-up call could be as simple as, "Good morning potential salesperson, do you like yourself?" But the issue is more profound than just liking yourself: it's about appreciating your own self-worth. It's about self-esteem. A professional salesperson, a professional motivator, must have a healthy amount of self-esteem. Self-esteem is the capacity to fully experience self-love and joy. This is not narcissism, but true value in self. From a deep sense of self-esteem comes a full appreciation of others. It's true! The appreciation of others is deeply routed in value derived from our own worth.

I believe this is the first step in developing one's mentality to be a salesperson: self-knowledge, self-appreciation, and a belief that who and what we are is worth sharing with other people. Now, let's rephrase the wake-up question: do I possess sufficient self-esteem? Is my sense of self-worth and belief in myself strong enough that I feel others would benefit by interacting with me? This self-examination calls for total honesty because of its serious implications for success or failure in a sales career, not to mention the frustration of not being able to consistently have things go your way even *for* the customer's benefit. Clearly, it is much easier and healthier to be one's true self than to invent a mask (be it one of Willy Loman or an interactive computer likeness) that will fool no one and perhaps have disappointing consequences. It's just plain common sense. The sales interaction is a sharing of who one is and what one has with another who accepts the same.

No one can share what he or she does not possess. No sharing, no interaction, and, certainly, no sale. Do I really want to share with others? If your answer is affirmative, you may be well on the road to becoming a salesperson. From this positive affirmation can flow a self-confidence based on the knowledge that you have an excellent chance to be successful in both your relationships with people and in your selling career.

In addition to the degree of self-confidence that follows from a healthy self-esteem, there also evolves the self-image that we bring to the world and, as salespeople, to our marketplace. The strength or weakness of this self-image is a true measure of self-esteem. Our image of self can be evaluated and enhanced at three basic but meaningful levels: physical (What really counts about my appearance?); mental (Do I use or abuse my mind?); and spiritual (Am I aware of my inner being, my soul?). However simplified these sound, they are profound questions and critical in ascertaining one's true self-image. These are an essential part of the wake-up call.

The Physical Self
Let's begin with the physical. It's no secret that the

world today is geared to "beautiful people." Good looks are bankable. They are an obsession with the media . . . a national addiction in a society that regards physical beauty far above its real value. All true. But maybe not so new. Three hundred years ago, the poet Dryden said, "None but the brave deserves the fair." Be that as it may, we must have a positive appreciation of our own physical appearance in order to have a self-image we can feel comfortable with. This is not to say that one has to be physically beautiful or pretend to be so. If you are a person who is not beautiful by television advertising standards, welcome to the club that includes most of your peers.

There are many ways to be beautiful physically aside from the soap-opera-culture definition of physical beauty, not the least of which is preserving your good health. While it isn't necessary to be a fitness fanatic, reasonable attention to good health results in a special physical radiance. A good diet, adequate rest, and exercise keep one feeling good and radiating a positive self-image. Weight limits should be realistic. Radiance and feeling good are more important than an inch or two. Let's not forget that selling in this context is an active vocation and, as such, requires that a salesperson be somewhat physically fit to meet the mental and physical demands of the job. Maintaining a reasonable physical profile combined with tasteful grooming and dress can greatly enhance your physical appearance and your image of yourself until you *radiate!* Your physical appearance should in no way deter your acceptance and interaction with others.

The Mental Self

From the standpoint of our self-image, nothing counts more than the mental assessment. We are our thoughts. We are more what we think than what we eat. Our thoughts lead us and *determine our destinies.*

This is clear when we consider the nature of the mind. While the mind is not an organ or muscle of the body, it is certainly a living thing and, as such, has vital needs. These needs are not unlike our bodily needs. And just as we feed and exercise our bodies so we must feed and exercise our minds. The food, our thoughts. If the mind is nourished on sub-par thoughts, its performance will be sub-par, weakened much like the body without exercise and good food. The measure of real self-love and appreciation is one's willingness to provide one's mind with good, healthy mental food. It should be a balanced and fresh diet. Just as we wouldn't think of feeding our bodies spoiled and decaying food, we shouldn't feed our minds worn-out thoughts or narrow viewpoints.

There seems to be a number of people whose mental development was curbed the day diplomas were given out. Education tapered where it should have begun. Successful salespersons, on the other hand, know how to use their minds and can think for themselves. They are independent and usually adept in conversing on a variety of topics and have balanced interests. Variety and balance are keys to avoiding extreme views that are the bane of the professional sales representative. To paraphrase one of Auntie Mame's famous lines, "Life is a smorgasbord of ideas. Pity the poor . . . who starve to death." These ideas come to us through an understanding and appreciation of literature, history, art, current events, various forms of entertainment, and reading materials that expose new ideas. They form the bedrock of a healthy, confident, and well-rounded mental attitude.

The Spiritual Self

The enjoyment of our spiritual being makes life worth living. We all know what our spiritual being is, but have difficulty with words that nail it. It's the soul, the heart, the inner being, our feelings . . . you know. In this context, we are not discussing church membership, religious preference, or philosophy, but rather the awareness of this inner being, our human spirit.

The true salesperson is a spiritual being, one who dreams and fantasizes, who appreciates great events and high principles much like the poets. In fact, the poet Robert Browning frames and phrases the question that all true salespersons ask themselves in one form or another:

> *Because a man has shop to mind*
> *In time and place, since flesh must live,*
> *Needs spirit lack all life behind,*
> *All stray thoughts, fancies fugitive*
> *All loves except what trade can give?*

It is a relevant question and the poet suggests a relevant and very human answer. Browning wants to know that, in their leisure hours, the butcher paints, the baker rhymes, and the candlestick-maker acquaints his soul with song. Browning understood that true growth is taking on the new, not repeating the old. He has this sad commentary: "Friend, your good angel slept . . . fate did you wrong."

His point is well made. There must be leisure time for one to relax her or his spirit — a time for total exhilaration unrelated to reason or practicality, a time to fulfill oneself and come into full possession of one's faculties, face to face with one's being as a whole. In enjoying leisure, we exercise fundamental powers of the human spirit that go beyond the task-oriented events of the workaday world to celebrate the creativity of our being. We are like multi-shaped snowflakes; the growing ones dream on each side of their shape. In so doing, we touch upon the superhuman life-giving powers that renew us emotionally and enable us to respond to life's events. The cathartic gift of tears at a movie or play or the exhilaration felt at the first touchdown in a high school football game are simple examples of how the spirit of living is captured in one's own being.

This spirit of living intensely can make one feel good about one's self, enhance self-image, and enrich the self one shares with the world. One needs to contemplate with visionary insight in order to keep in touch with one's spirituality, to ensure that one continues to be capable of seeing life as a whole and the world as a whole. This is an imperative for anyone who would become a complete salesperson, since the person who does not dream and fantasize the realization of those dreams is probably not destined to become a sales hero.

Your Magnetism
If you check out even potentially "okay" on these

physical, mental and spiritual paradigms, you will have no need to reinvent yourself each morning to face the world. You will know yourself, believe in yourself, and like yourself.

What does this mean to your career? Think of the last time you felt the presence of a magnetic personality in a room full of people. Such a person may have been so charismatic that all were aware of her or his presence because, without even speaking, that person emitted vibes that the crowd seemed to pick up instinctively. Natural human genius for people shining forth? Perhaps. But, believe me, in 99 out of 100 such scenes, there is nothing really godly or mystical about that person. To be sure, it's extraordinary. He or she is simply displaying a positive self-image and a liking for self and others.

People who have high self-esteem radiate that magnetism from the twinkle in their eyes to the intensity of their gaits. Their very presence makes you feel good about being near the same space. They like themselves and are certain that anyone who comes in contact with them will like and respect them. And it's usually true.

The customer is quick to recognize such salespersons as unique and appealing in their ways, a critical perception since the customer has neither the time nor the will to deal with a salesperson whose personality or mood seems to change with the weather. The customer needs to know, like, and trust the real you. Hence, the importance of the wake-up call is to get you in touch with your creative, visionary self. You'll like it . . . and so will everyone else.

More Tools

At this point, I trust you would agree that your progress in self-awareness should be an integral part of your self-development. Through psychology or other relevant courses, you may already have valuable insights into your personality and your ability to achieve self-actualization. All the better if you are in sales as a result of such self-study. On the other hand, if you have not had a recent in-depth personality assessment, you can arrange to get such feedback on yourself by contacting a college career counseling service. Local community colleges usually offer a variety of such tests. This exercise and its results may help you with the basic "Who am I?" query.

And, while you are at it, you might inquire about the college's drama classes. There is no better way to discover and develop the range of your emotional portfolio than through acting classes. Sales heroes must possess the self-discipline to care, which involves a wide repertoire of emotional skills.

Remember: the core of the selling dialogue is always emotional. It is by using and controlling our emotions within that dialogue that we have the power to motivate others for our mutual benefit.

2. The Elements of Motivational Selling

First guess a man's ruling passion, appeal to it by word. Find out each man's thumb-screw. . . . All men are idolaters; some of fame, others of self-interest, most of pleasure. Skill consists in knowing these idols in order to bring them into play. Knowing any man's mainspring of motive, you will have . . . the key to his will.

B. Gracian, 1643

Read "hotbutton" for "thumbscrew" and this 300-year-old observation on the art of persuasion is as good an anatomy of the motivational sale as you will find anywhere! It has everything: the motivator, the motives, and the motivated, plus insight into what must happen from a human standpoint for a selling transaction to proceed to a successful conclusion. In addition, it points up the unchanging quality of human nature. From mankind's beginning, the basic emotions, i.e., love and hate, desire or dislike, pleasure and pain, hope, fear, anger, and so on have been powers inherent in humans that help them attain what they perceive as good or avoid what they perceive as bad for them. All human initiative springs from these powerful emotions, since they drive all desire.

How do these emotions translate into the motives that propel the selling process? To catalog all the possible specific motives for a sale would require a book of dictionary proportions. For this reason, I have identified two basic, global motives for purchasing goods and services.

Self-Esteem

The first of these motives is enhancement of self-esteem, based on pursuit of what is perceived as good for the individual and what makes one feel better about one's self. The tangible and intangible objects that people pursue for the enhancement of their own self-esteem are like so many mirrors giving back to them pictures of who and what they are or what they want to be in their heart of hearts.

As a reason for buying, self-esteem enhancement encompasses all the powerful acquisitive motives such as pride, fame and fortune, love and pleasure, and all variations of self-interest. Enhancement of self-esteem is the operative motive in the person who rushes out to buy the latest version of the Cabbage Patch fad doll as well as the physician who has just prescribed the latest pain-relieving wonder drug for an arthritic patient. While there is no comparison between the two from the perspective of value, these examples underscore how enhancement of one's self-esteem results in feelings of pleasure or joy in self when a decision perceived as good is made. The positive pictures of self that are reflected back to the impulse buyer and the physician are very self-satisfying. Positive fantasy of self is greatly enhanced by the decision to purchase this product.

Remote Control

It is worth noting here that the selling/buying process in the purchase of the latest fad is in a different genre than the motivational selling process we are examining. I call it *selling by remote control*. In the first example, the toy store cashier who rings up the sale at point of purchase is an incidental figure in the transaction. The creator of the fad and the advertising people who put together the product's compelling media profile were the real salespeople. They pushed all the right buttons. In planning their tactics, these motivators knew that the overpowering drive to acquire confers status when the buyer can tell others that he or she is in possession of a popular item. Had this purchase required a selling dialogue, the motivational salesperson would have used the same emotional appeal to self-esteem. Mass marketing and personal selling do not share the same bed all the time, but in these examples the enhancement of self-esteem is the basic motive for buying.

Subtle Fear

A second powerful buying motive is subtle fear.

The basic cause of fear is the concern that something will deprive a person of a perceived good. *Subtle* is the key word in describing this motive since the injection of cold, stark fear into a selling dialogue is paralyzing and counterproductive. Furthermore, extreme dramatic fear has a life of its own, and people react to it very unpredictably. Subtle fear gets as much attention as enhancement of self-esteem but usually in planned "free choice" decision-oriented scenarios.

Subtle fear is the motivator much of the time in professional selling. Insurance companies have parlayed the fear of leaving loved ones unprotected in the event of death into one of the most lucrative industries in the world. Insurance agents utilize subtle fear at every level of the insurance sale dialogue. As a buying motive, subtle fear is not confined to this industry but is employed by sales professionals across the board to sell products that do not determine life or death. How often we hear subtle fear phrases such as, "You'd better hurry up and buy because we expect shortages next year," or the classic phrase originally used to sell a brand of oil filter, "You can pay me now . . . or pay me later." The appeal is the same: "What will happen to me if I do not have the product?"

Subtle fear, put another way, manifests itself as the strong desire for peace of mind in each of us. We're very uncomfortable when something that is within our control slips out of that tight circle. Professional salespeople recognize this and position their products within the buyer's comfort zone, thus ensuring the peace of mind that comes with the buyer's retaining control.

Fear as a buying motive should never be presented too dramatically, since dramatic fear often provokes unpredictable, unreliable decisions. Fear motivation should never be a frontal attack on the customer; it's simply a word picture describing the presence or absence of peace of mind hinging on possession of the product or service. Remember, fear as a motivating factor must be *subtle*.

Anyone who has ever been through a basic sales course has run the gamut of the feature, advantage, benefit scenario. As a result, most salespeople correctly subscribe to the slogan "Benefit selling is the only selling." It's doubtful that most understand that good benefit selling has two essential elements. The first is, "Look how much better off you will be and how much your self-worth will be enhanced if you buy the product." That's enhancement of self-esteem. And the second is, "Look at the peace of mind you will have by buying this product." Not having the product or service will mean absence of peace of mind. That's the heart of subtle fear motivation. Salespeople who understand the dynamics of subtle fear motivation know how to coalesce services and products with the potential customer's needs.

Subtle fear may sound like an intimidating term, or even a manipulative or devious one. In this context, however, it certainly is not. As human beings, each of us possesses an array of hidden and not-so-hidden fears. The salesperson who can relieve these fears and bring us peace of mind is indeed a welcome friend who should be sought out for a business or even a personal relationship.

If subtle fear is employed correctly in the selling scenario, it demonstrates a sincere caring for the customer. Again, the human factor. The salesperson who motivates another using subtle fear is saying, "I care about your peace of mind, and what I'm selling will assist in your task and reduce your anxiety level." The salesperson who motivates with subtle fear based on truth cares about the customer. He or she is a caring individual. Unfortunately, enhancement of self-esteem and subtle fear motivators can be employed by cynical, dishonest individuals to manipulate and threaten the well-being of the customer. True salespersons neither embellish nor distort these motivators for an immediate, short-term, dishonest, selfish gain.

The Dance

It is clear that strong emotions are ever-present motives in the selling/buying behavior on both sides of the sales dialogue. This is what makes the selling process such a highly charged human interface. Never forget it. Even when seller and buyer meet under ideal circumstances, they attempt to "do a number on each other."

Salesperson and customer attempt to prove to each other that they are logical, truth-oriented, and trustworthy to the extent that they would never sell or buy anything except the best product for the best reasons at the best price with perfect timing. Each looks for an opening or moment of vulnerability to press home some aspect of this viewpoint. To all appearances everything is reasonable and rational. In fact, the buyer may even have a long list of logical reasons that must be fulfilled as a condition for her or his decision to purchase.

As the selling process proceeds, the salesperson listens to what the customer says, empathizes with needs, observes closely how the buyer processes benefits information, and searches for the buyer's areas of vulnerability. Throughout, the good salesperson is looking to discover the emotional "hotbutton" that will motivate a favorable final decision for both parties. If all goes well and a strong desire to purchase emerges, the buyer begins to feel the emotional satisfaction that comes with the finality of making a good decision, and the sale is made.

Clearly, this selling/buying experience is as uniquely human as a dance. People buy from people with whom they have a relationship, no matter how fundamental or elementary that relationship may be. If the products to be purchased are in the same relative value area, you can be sure that "people things" take over, proving the truth of the old adage, "people buy from people." Many pitfalls in the sales interaction can be avoided if the salesperson has a sound understanding of emotional motivation: When a sale is made, someone has motivated another to act in her or his behalf in the emotional mode. The transaction should be mutually beneficial.

3. The Customer as a Person

First, all selling calls must focus on the customer. All that is said and done must be perceived by the customer as appropriate and advantageous to her or his self-interest. If the customer senses that a call is a performance by a salesperson to display her or his own vast skill and knowledge, the sales call will fall into the category of "good presentation, but no sale." Further, delivering a well-articulated presentation that is not person-oriented can cause irreparable damage to the relationship.

Billy L. Skinner
(talk to sales trainees, 1976)

Unfortunately, variations of this type of Teflon sales call are legion. They range from the cool informa-tion-as-agent-of-change approach so favored by many sales managers who should know better, to the staccato, strident pitch of the car salesman in Robin Williams' *Cadillac Man*. But all Teflon sales calls have a common denominator: they ignore the cus-tomer as a person. Most customers, including you and I, tend to be unforgiving when "done" this way. While we rarely complain openly to the salesperson when we're treated as objects, we sure know how to punish such behavior. A few of us, however, do com-plain. Consider the plight of the salesman who expressed surprise at the cold shoulder he was get-ting from one of his best customers. In response to his query as to why, the customer reminded him of his previous sales call. "You came in here with anoth-er gentleman, your manager. You were different. You acted like he was some kind of god and I existed for the two of you. I listened to your canned presenta-tion of everything I already knew about your prod-ucts only because I thought we were friends. Now I'm not so sure and I'm still angry." That's a very hurt person as well as a "hurting" salesperson.

Remember the first rule of motivational sell-ing from the opening chapter: Be yourself with all that it means in terms of your own self-image and self-esteem. The risk is worth it. Its corollary is to always treat and respect the customer as a person who has the same self-image and self-esteem needs as you do. Acting naturally instead of playing a role inspires in your customers a special kind of trust and connectedness. You violate these cardinal rules of motivational selling at your own peril and the peril of the cause or product you are selling.

Person-oriented Selling

Selling is personalism in action, so it is understandable that sales managers constantly urge sales professionals to be people-oriented. They often add the refrain, "You gotta' sell yourself first." These phrases, though somewhat overused, have profound meaning. More often, in both oral and written communications, they are used in a superficial way that overlooks the dual nature (seller/buyer) as well as the personal nature of the selling process. For many sales managers, "people-oriented" conjures up a talkative, ever-smiling extrovert who is generally well-mannered and considerate of his fellow human beings. As human behavior, this is not bad, but as a facade recommended to ensure the closing of a sale, it is just not good enough. In this sense, people-oriented seems self-centered, one-sided, like something that can be practiced in front of a mirror. I prefer "person-oriented" to "people-oriented." Unlike the generic, collective noun *people*, person-oriented signifies that the professional motivator must be sensitive to the uniquely personal nature of the selling interface as well as have some understanding of the person to be sold. Person-oriented recognizes that the selling dialogue is a two-sided process that can be practiced only in the real world.

Similarly, the "You gotta' sell yourself first" admonition had better mean more than hail-fellow-well-met. As noted earlier, the true salesperson is well-grounded in physical, mental, and spiritual fun-

THE SOUL OF SELLING

damentals, because these constitute the self-image he or she projects to the real world. Your responsibility as a salesperson is to make sure you are salable in a way that makes your customer shine. If a customer accepts you as a good and trustworthy person with whom to do business, that confidence should be rewarded many times over by your intense interest in her or his personhood as well as with good products and services. This combination of genuine interest and good products and services reinforces the customer's belief that her or his judgment is very sound indeed.

Why such a focused discussion of people-oriented versus person-oriented, self-directed versus other-directed, one-sided versus two-sided, practice in front of a mirror versus practice in the real world? It's more than just semantics. Too much lip service is given to customer orientation while the customer is ignored as a person. Too many people in sales think that the object of the sales dialogue is to bring the customer into the salesperson's comfort zone. No thought is given to the customer's comfort zone or the automatic defenses that go up when it's threatened. This world-according-to-me approach holds that in order to make a sale the salesperson must win over the customer to her or his point of view since the actual sale takes place in the salesperson's world: "I know you and what it takes to make you happy. Just listen to me and I'll make a believer and a buyer out of you." If this to-know-me-is-to-love-me approach sounds familiar, it's because as customers we have been treated this way so often.

The Comfort Zone

Tom Peters, management expert and author, notes those companies that achieve excellence are those whose sales performers are "really close" to their customers. He adds wryly that the intensity of person orientation in these top companies is "one of the best kept secrets in American business." The true salesperson knows that the sale takes place in and around the customer's comfort zone and that to motivate a person to act aggressively in one's behalf requires the ability to understand and work within that person's comfort zone.

At the heart of every customer's comfort zone is a highly developed personal value system. Nurtured and reinforced over a lifetime, this value system draws on the socio-economic, political, religious, and aesthetic aspects of life (and the corporate culture) to shape the way we think, feel, and act. In addition to defining who we are, our value system is the source of those emotion-driven attitudes that predispose us to act in a certain way. The world of customer attitudes, grounded in emotional perceptions, is where the professional salesperson lives. These attitudes, often offered as the rational basis for or against a buying decision, are emotional biases that can present a real challenge to the salesperson, especially when they are long-held and often-rewarded.

The Emotional Bank Account

To motivate someone to act on your behalf for her or his own benefit, you must build a relationship with that customer as a person. You must bond with that person's value system to better understand and appreciate the emotional underpinnings of her or his values and attitudes. As one sales hero noted, "The salesperson opens an emotional bank account" with each customer. Continuous small deposits will ensure that withdrawals are covered. It's a sound analogy and, as we shall see, is operative from day one of the seller-buyer relationship.

At no point in the seller-buyer relationship is the salesperson more vulnerable than in those critical initial contacts with a new customer. Most of the old clichés about the importance of first impressions are true: First impressions are self-perpetuating, hard if not impossible to undo with words, and can be the beginning of the end of the relationship. (You never get a second chance to make a first impression.) (Thank you, Head & Shoulders.) Knowing this and knowing how he or she wants to be perceived, the true salesperson puts her or his "best foot forward" on those first calls, fully aware that the all-important non-verbal aspects of that first contact will be fully scrutinized by the prospective customer. It's understandable. The customer wants to get a "handle" on this salesperson: We are looking for an inner voice to tell us whether or not this person fits the okay-for-me-to-do-business-with pattern or not. It's a natural form of stereotyping that humans use so that they will know how to react in various interpersonal situations. Do they make mistakes in snap judgments about individual salespeople? Of course they do — plenty and with lightning speed. That's the inherent danger in all stereotyping, but it's real. In pursuit of the good stereotype label, the wary salesperson approaches all initial sales calls on new customers with the respect and trepidation of a first-time highwire artist.

The common ground in these initial person-perception exchanges is the mutual "aliveness" of seller and buyer — aliveness meaning projected interest in each other and in the scenario, and how anxious each is to project or conquer "turf." Initially, these first encounters are silent, wordless tests of the intensity and depth of the aliveness of both parties in each other's presence. Both parties want to know how much of a personal stake each has in this encounter and how much turf each one is expected to give up. As a sales manager, my gentle reminder to sales representatives, especially on first time calls, has always been, "Remember you are dealing with a real, live person. That person gets up in the morning, does a number of humbling things, shares the same environment, and has similar concerns about job, family, and future as you do. Don't insult that person's need for self-esteem by showing anything less than your genuine pleasure at being alive in her or his company. And, if you take turf or give it, make sure it's a good trade emotionally." That is, both parties are happy to be participating in the interaction.

Reading Between the Lines

This positive signal is often returned in kind. The message exchanges of facial expressions and eye contact are dominant factors in communication. In an instant, countenances can share the enjoyment of each other's presence. Eye contact that is vibrant portends interesting conversations to follow and an exchange of friendly smiles can promote sealing the first-impression bargaining.

This may be the ideal, but be assured it is very doable within the framework of a motivational selling approach. Reading facial emotions is a two-way street between salesperson and customer and, since value systems are in large part emotion-driven, it is an essential first step in the bridge-building process. Just how essential is underscored in an article titled "Where Emotions Come From," which appeared in *U.S. News and World Report.* An M.I.T. neuroscientist, commenting on an auto accident victim's loss of his ability to read faces, notes, "People who can't recognize facial emotions feel like they can't read between the lines, and there's a tremendous awkwardness in relating to other people."

While this uncanny ability to read between the lines persists throughout a relationship, the brain's built-in "software" is nowhere more evident than in the non-verbal formation of first impressions. Once friendly smiles and gestures are exchanged, and perhaps discounted, the customer's non-verbal probe focuses squarely on the salesperson's social-emotional style, knowing instinctively that this style is the signature of her or his value system (*Le style est l'homme même*). The reading of this signature is as practical and pragmatic as it is automatic and instantaneous, to wit: intentions (what do you want from me?), similarities (how are you like me?), dissimilarities (how are you unlike me?), and even relative social status.

Since the customer knows why the salesperson is there, this first quick read of the salesperson's intentions is a measure of her or his trustworthiness. Is he or she a good person? Intent is from the heart. Good intent is the foundation of solid relationships. At this early stage, the similarity probe can part the waves for the salesperson since similarity is the main reason why people are attracted to one another: "to be like is to be liked." It means shared value systems and a ready insight into the attitudes and intentions that predispose another to act in a certain way.

Dissimilarities, on the other hand, can present a real problem in the initial impression phase especially when they are interpreted as character flaws — mistakenly or not. Fortunately, in many cases, differences are not extreme and, though recorded, may be overlooked by mature customers. In some instances, certain differences can create a positive first impression by establishing one's uniqueness in such a way as to rouse the potential customer's curiosity.

Clearly, the first impressions we make on others are influenced more by looks and body talk than by what we say. Each of us has a characteristic way of signaling our "vibes" to the outside world by the faces we wear, our posture, gestures, grooming, and the host of subtle overtones and undertones that accompany every move we make. Taken together, they all add up to something as personal and unique as a signature, and to the customer it seems to be a reliable insight into the salesperson's character. Intuition puts all these non-verbal messages together and presents the customer with a mental "printout," which, in turn, is used to determine reward or punishment. Is it any wonder that a high degree of social courage is the hallmark of the successful salesperson?

Certainly, actions more than words shape initial impressions. As the relationship matures, the information content of the sales message takes on somewhat more importance, but the salesperson continues to be judged more on actions than words. To information-age sales trainers, who spend 80 percent of their budgets on programs that emphasize product knowledge, this type of thinking may seem outside the mainstream. As one sales trainer put it, "Give me a good features, benefits selling story any day and spare me the agony and the ecstasy." Give me a hard close without all the touchy-feely people stuff!

The pervasiveness of this type of thinking calls for a re-examination of what so-called "mainstreamers" are doing to our young sales trainees. Remember Tom Peters' previously quoted observation that true person orientation as practiced by a handful of top companies is one of American business' "best-kept secrets." Again, no one is questioning the need for thorough product knowledge per se. Sound product knowledge must be a given for the professional salesperson. Anything less is unethical as well as counterproductive. There is a tendency for customer turnoff when confronted with an uninformed salesperson. But the objective of selling is to motivate and, by themselves, facts don't motivate or change behavior. Facts without passion have no compelling persuasive value. They tend to be distorted to fit the customer's existing value system.

There is just no way to get around it: The selling dialogue takes place within an emotional framework that is an essential part of the sales message. In the selling context, language is the reinforcer par excellence. It can help solidify attitudes already held by customers and can give them phrases they can use to express their strongly held feelings in support of a product or service. It is an excellent vehicle for new information on products or a totally new innovation or idea. Just don't expect language to bear the full burden of responsibility for the success or failure of the sales call.

Cultivating Empathy

As an active participant in this exchange of first perceptions, the salesperson, like the customer, sizes up the other person in much the same ways. Understandably, there is more urgency on the part of the salesperson in this exchange, since success depends on her or his ability to understand and bond with the customer's value system. As we shall see, there are many working theories that aid us in assessing customer value systems. However, no amount of speculation on how customers process values will help the salesperson who is incapable of identifying with those values. This ability to share in another's feelings is called *empathy*, which Webster defines as "the capacity for participating in another's feelings or ideas." You will recall an earlier recommendation to attend drama classes when and where possible. It was not made lightly or with the notion that a good salesperson must be a good actor. Drama is the artistic expression of empathy. Robert DeNiro is the great actor he is not because he is good at playing well-memorized parts, but because the depth and breadth of his ability to empathize with the characters he portrays makes them come to life for us. In similar fashion, the good salesperson empathizes her or his way into the attitude and value system of every customer in the territory. The bad news is that there is only one DeNiro. The good news is that this ability to empathize with others is a shared human faculty that can be cultivated and improved with practice and through experience.

Practicing empathy is an exercise in caring. And while empathy is operative every moment in our face-to-face encounters with others, it also contributes to our vision of how we will act towards them in future meetings. Empathy identifies similarities in value systems. Bonding with people through similarities inspires the behavioral adjustments required to complete the sale. Empathy *cum laude* rather than "the gift of gab" characterizes the really great sales heroes.

How do we assess another person's value system? Rule one is that no detail about the customer or the company is extraneous. Everything should be regarded as highly important intelligence information. Harvey Mackay, super-salesperson and author, puts knowing everything about your customer on a par with knowing everything about your product. He maintains a 66-item written profile on each of his customers that covers everything from nickname to special interests and lifestyles.

Moral and ethical considerations in the customer relationship are also part of the customer profile. The information for this profile comes from the customers, newspapers, trade publications, receptionists and secretaries. It makes good sense to collect such information since you have to know something about someone before you can begin to empathize with that person. If a company's official customer profile confines itself to business statistics, the enterprising salesperson compiles a customized profile to include those personal items that determine attitudes and values.

The most valuable customer profile contains useful factual (demographic) as well as psychological (psychographic) information that will help the salesperson access the customer's attitude and value system. Simply stated, demographics refer to the finite characteristics of populations that are easily defined and measurable, i.e. age, sex, income, education, product use or non-use, and other statistics.

Psychographics refers to those not-so-easy-to-measure attitudes and values that stem from the buyer's psychological make-up. Using basic elements of readily available demographic and psychographic information, the "tuned-in" salesperson creates conceptual models for each customer, which open windows on how that customer will react in certain buying situations, including the adoption of new products. The salesperson fashions these working, predictive models to better influence or modify buying behavior, not to create judgmental stereotypes for their own sake.

One such important model is the maturation grid (see Figure 1), which is time-related and can be defined in terms of chronological age. *Maturation*, as defined by Webster, is the emergence of personal characteristics and behavioral phenomena through growth processes. These stages of life, though beyond our control, are powerful influences on how

FIGURE 1: **Maturation Grid**

STAGE	
Content (ages 65-beyond)	Products must accent contentment benefits. Do not oversell.
Creative (ages 41-65)	Products must accent adaptive and creative benefits.
Mature (ages 17-40)	Products must accent the ripening process — symmetry.
Growth (birth to ages 15-16)	Products must be interpreted in terms of getting more or bigger.

we assimilate and process value. For sales purposes, this maturation process can be broken down into four stages:

1. **Growth** (birth to age 15–16). During this period of growing, hormone-driven mental and physical changes are dramatic, occur with the rapidity of seasonal changes, and are often accompanied by environmental changes, new schools, new friends, and, as always, new wardrobes. People in this first compartment of environmental existence create and process their values in terms of this explosive growth. If you want to communicate with someone in this stage, be prepared to speak to and empathize with the growing process. Your product should be positioned to benefit by its "growth."

2. **Mature** (age 17–40). The mature stage, or young adulthood, has two parts. Its beginning is

marked by intense activity as well as major life decisions. In a relatively short period of time, one can graduate into the world, start a career, marry, become a parent, and build a first home. All this can happen in a period of 60 months or less! In part two of the mature phase, the results of many of these earlier decisions begin to come to fruition, analogous to the fruit ripening on the vine or the dream coming true — maturing, if you will. If people want to sell us concepts and products during this period they must appeal to us as builders of realistic dreams and bountiful harvests. Empathetic focus is on making dreams come true and the ripening process — the tomato turning red.

3. **Creative** (age 41–65). During this period, the nature of our creativity changes and we must adapt sometimes to the process of some deterioration. This is not as pejorative as it sounds, nor does it mean that individuals in this stage of life are falling apart. Keep in mind that a grid is a conceptual reference. Its stated aim is non-logical because it targets all important emotional values based on age segmentation. People in the creative stage of life are comfortable building on what has gone before and adapting to what may be happening in their lives. They have been there and "done it." They may encourage others in the creative stage to avail themselves of the new generation of ideas, for example, "You have computers, we had plastics."

As noted, during this period people are often faced with the first of what can be a series of personal setbacks: deaths of family members or friends, major illness, job loss, divorce, and problems with adult children that can be devastating. The reality of this deterioration process factors itself into our value systems at this time and, whether we like it or not, becomes operative in how we assimilate and process values. Empathetic appeals to this group should focus on what it yearns for most, perhaps contentment derived from having "done it" and an offering to assist in adapting to new life events.

4. **Content** (age 65 and beyond). In this maturity stage of life, we must factor our own mortality into our thinking. While this is a time of more conscious thoughts about the inevitable, it need not be a period of babbling despair as portrayed in the play *Waiting for Godot*. During this stage, there is a good deal of reflection and the expressed need to feel our lives have been marked by definite accomplishments that identify us as worthy. Values during this last phase of life are shaped by these kinds of needs. Sentimental, nostalgic appeals have special empathetic meaning for this group. Do not oversell with this group. Place your wares in the mode of an understanding wisdom that somehow contents!

The maturation grid is a useful tool that helps the salesperson think about emotional selling approaches within the various age segments. Still, it is not refined enough, in most selling situations, to type the inner needs of the value systems that motivate individual prospects. Shared demographics are a reference, not a predictor, of how values are assimilated and needs satisfied. For this, the salesperson must be sensitive to how the buyer processes values based on her or his inner value assimilator. In his classic work on American lifestyles, Arnold Mitchell notes, "More than anything else, we are what we believe, what we dream, what we value. For the most part, we try to mold our lives to make our beliefs and dreams, come true."

To identify with the customer's beliefs, dreams, and values is the salesperson's ultimate challenge. It's the job. In so doing, he or she encounters and deals directly with a variety of customer value-processing modes. To create a conceptual grid, I have identified four basic value-processing modes (see Figure 2). Again, this is not an attempt to identify personality types or to create stereotypes for their own sake. We all operate

FIGURE 2: **Value-Processing Modes**

Self-esteemed Does it expand my horizons?	**Self-actualized** Does it make me a better, more developed person?
Fair-minded Is it fair and balanced?	**Self-centered** What's in it for me?

primarily in one of these modes and may cross over into another from time to time:

The Self-Centered: Those who chronically process value out of this ego-driven, self-oriented mode ("What's in it for me?") are interested primarily in things that gratify self immediately if not sooner. This behavior is easily recognized and typed because all of us have acted out of this mode at one time or another.

But there is a difference between the normal-occasional and the consistent-narcissistic. Whereas the normal person can laugh retrospectively at the vanity of a foolish action or purchase, the totally self-centered individual is dead serious about anything that pleasures or glorifies her or his inner being. Unfortunately, narcissism infects the brilliant and the bold. The importance of the salesperson and her or his product or service is inversely proportionate to the self-centered customer's ego needs. Salesperson and product can be "very small" indeed. Still, it's what is going on in the customer's head that counts since the customer's perception creates the reality. To make this sale, the salesperson may end up persuading the customer that the product or service was the customer's idea in the first place. For such a customer, vanity fair is an everyday event.

The Fair-Minded: Customers who process value in this mode have internal and external assurance needs. Internally, they are confident of their own sense of what is fair and true. Externally, they must have assurances of the justice ("Is it fair?") and truth ("Don't ever lie to me or we're finished!") of any proposal or product. Instinctively they demand that fairness and truth be an essential element of all business transactions and relationships.

This mind-set is familiar to all of us. If you borrow $50 from me with the promise to pay it back, the money still belongs to me even though you have the use of it. Refusal to pay it back is unjust and dishonest. In the selling situation, the fair-minded customer may insist that the only fair price is the lowest price, whereas the truth may be that the lowest-priced product may not be totally cost-effective or beneficial in other value areas. In this case, the fair-minded customer would reject the lowest-priced product as no longer "fair." This value system processes all things in terms of fairness and truth: an eye for an eye.

The Self-Esteemed: Self-esteem was defined earlier as the capacity for healthy self-love and joy. From a deep sense of self-esteem comes a full appreciation of others. The customer who processes value in the self-esteemed mode is committed to judging value in terms of fairness and truth with an added humanistic consideration: love and appreciation of fellow humans and the human condition. It may sound strange but it's true.

Once again, consider the selling situation cited at the beginning of this chapter. The customer resented being ignored while being used as a sounding board for the salesman's canned presentation to impress his boss. The customer didn't mind sitting still for the canned presentation because, as he said, "I thought we were friends." He was willing to do this out of friendship without expecting anything tangible in return. To be insulted in return for his good deed was the "mega-hurt." Nevertheless, this customer was obviously looking for a way to forgive the salesperson or he wouldn't have mentioned the hurt.

Obviously, the self-esteemed are the jewels in the crown of any good sales territory. These are very interesting people who, when satisfied that a cause is fair and true, will go the extra mile with the salesperson to assure general acceptance. These are the people who, when all things are equal, will factor your friendship and good service into the buying decision. They will forgive you for being who you are. Nurture them!

The Self-Actualized: These are the exceptional few who are well on their way to realizing their full potential as human beings. They process value on its own merits without regard to what others may say or think. Self-actualized persons defy liberal or conservative labels and they cannot be characterized by lifestyle. They live beyond labels because they are unique. Since they see change as part of living, they are excited by new people as well as new concepts. They form relationships with people who are extremely different from them. They are not afraid to accept and act on proven new concepts. In sum, the self-actualized are in tune with the world and with living. They are the few free. Their sense of self-worth and the worth of others is unshakable. They are the superstars!

As useful as the maturation grid and value-processing modes are in helping the salesperson bond with the customer's value system, they are equally valuable in identifying customers who would be the most likely to try newly introduced products.

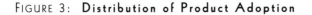

FIGURE 3: **Distribution of Product Adoption**

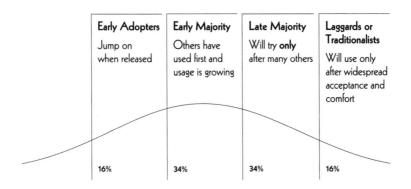

Early Adopters	Early Majority	Late Majority	Laggards or Traditionalists
Jump on when released	Others have used first and usage is growing	Will try **only** after many others	Will use only after widespread acceptance and comfort
16%	34%	34%	16%

To appreciate *how* valuable, one need only examine the adopter quadrants of the bell-shaped distribution curve in Figure 3. Studies indicate that the distribution of product adoption by customers generally follows this curve:

Early Adopters: People in this group are willing to try new products when they are first released. They are likely to be in the creative stage of life and, although their motives may differ widely, process value in either the self-centered or self-actualized mode.

Early Majority: People in this group are willing to try after others have used and usage appears to be growing. They are likely to be in the late-mature, early-creative stage of life and process value in the self-esteemed mode.

47

Late Majority: Those in this group are skeptical and will try only after many others — they require much persuasion. They are likely to be in the content stage of life and process value in the fair-minded mode.

Laggards or Traditionalists: Those in this group will try only after wide usage — even wider usage than people in the late majority category. They are generally in the late-content stage of life and process value in the fair-minded mode, like late majority consumers.

Good salespeople have always used some sort of conceptual models to bond with the value systems of their customers. Once bonded, the true salesperson is an interpreter of value. To visualize this, think of customers' attitudes and value systems as created, emotion-driven vehicles. Using enhancement of self-esteem and subtle fear, the prime motivators discussed in Chapter 2, the salesperson fashions psychological drivers for those vehicles. The key is understanding the nature of the vehicle and putting the right psychological driver in the vehicle to make it go for you. This analogy makes it sound easy, but I assure you it takes an enormous amount of skill and practice to perfect this talent.

We've compiled three grids so far, charts that you might bear in mind as you practice evaluating your prospect's attitudes and needs. Is this person predominantly narcissistic, or more self-actualized? Is he or she an eager experimenter or more skeptical when it comes to trying a new product? Is he or she closer to the creative stage of life or the content stage? As you take this holistic view of the person and what may motivate him or her — determining which modes of operation are at work — you may find these classifications overlapping; you may discover tendencies, shown in the chart on page 75 (Chapter 5). Remember, however, people are individuals, and don't always fit into the neat slots we've devised for them. But with careful evaluation and interpretation of each individual's perceptions, you may be able to meet the ultimate challenge of sales: identifying with your customer.

4. Long-Term Relationships: Human Dynamics

It's easier to keep an account than it is to regain one. Easier, that is, if your orientation is long-term relationships. And the basis for an enduring association is, of course, understanding and concern. A company [salesperson] that views a business relationship strictly from a selfish vantage point has no right to expect loyalty from the other principal. I don't see how you can be successful in the long run if the customer isn't strengthened by his involvement with you.

F. G. "Buck" Rodgers

Not long ago, I ran into a national sales manager whose company had just divided its sales force into three separate divisions based on product specialties. "Brilliant move," he said. "Think of the increased market penetration in each of our territories. We all know that the average salesperson makes a living off about 10 percent to 15 percent of the territory's population. Now, at the very least, we'll be doing business with an additional 20 percent to 30 percent in each territory." The percentages are about right, and he is right. He elaborated, "I'm a firm believer in the old adage 'to be like is to be liked,' and it really works in sales.

"Unfortunately, too many of our sales people never go beyond those customers they like and who like them. I've been on many a sales call where customer and salesperson are like friends and you know it's a win-win situation. But too often I've seen that very same veteran salesperson go through what I call the 'let's-pretend-we're-not-people' selling exchange.

"In the absence of real relationships, many salespersons are petrified that customers will reject them for whatever reasons — fear of a tough question, fear of the customer's higher social status. Often, this fear reflects the salesperson's own prejudice; that is, the customer does not look, think, or behave according to the salesperson's value system — so, the old not-like-is-not-to-like takes over. So what happens? They give monotonous, pre-set presentations that invite little or no customer participation, and they can't wait to say, 'Thank you and goodbye.' They flee and falsely hope that the business will come. It never does unless the customer is already sold and the monotone serves as a boring commercial. So, my friend, there is no place in professional sales for 'let's-pretend-we're-not-people' people who cop-out on the firing line."

Expanding Your Horizons

Agreed. The true professional salesperson does not limit her or his customer base to so-called friends. In fact, expanding one's customer base is a most exciting and challenging aspect of sales because it draws on the intelligence as well as every facet of the salesperson's personality; it is critical to a successful selling career. Whereas the run-of-the-mill salesperson tends to write off the customer who says, "I don't like your company, your products or, for that matter, you," the real pro will likely thank that customer for being so open and frank. At the same time, in the mind's eye, the real pro looks forward to the day when that same customer will do a 180° turn and be thankful that the salesperson is there to help fulfill the newly perceived self-esteem or peace of mind need. This happens more often than you might think.

Ask any successful salesperson of your acquaintance how she or he deals with this seemingly total rejection and the response will be much the same: "It gets the adrenaline going, and you can't wait to turn the situation into a positive one for sales." Are sales heroes masochists or what? Not at all. Their reactions are acts of a practical courage that stems from a high degree of self-confidence and self-esteem. They are like Olympic athletes who courageously endure the pain and sacrifice of long hours of practice and yet gladly risk all in a brief moment of vulnerability before a world audience. The analogy is apt. The star sales performer knows that great rewards and recognition follow on hard work and high risk, so he or she welcomes vulnerability in order to develop those long-term relationships so essential for success.

Courage, then, is a hallmark of successful salespeople because that's how they become self-made heroes. Courage is about conquering fear. It involves overcoming difficulties and taking risks to achieve personal goals. Psychologists tell us that fear of loud noises and falling are the only two fears we are born with. All the rest are acquired responses. That's the good news. If acquired, they can be conquered and changed. In the process of building customer relationships, the cause of fear is usually within the salesperson — her or his real or imagined weaknesses. Therefore, the totally unprepared salesperson has every reason to fear that the sales call will end in dismal failure.

A *Friend in Need*

Establishing a long-term relationship within the selling framework means creating a state of interdependence between you and the customer. In addition to giving up something of yourself, it means taking the time, making the good effort, and, yes, having the courage to get to know, like, and win the trust of as many individual customers as possible within the territory. It's a tall order. Not the order executed by a majority of salespeople who often act as though selling begins with the first spoken words of the sales presentation and ends with the completion of the call report. If anything, pre-call planning means little more than scanning a visual aid or verifying a customer's location. The majority of salespeople never address or plan for the customer's personhood.

No amount of outward friendliness can overcome this negative approach, which customers are quick to sense and determined to punish by with-holding commitment and action. Real pros know that their customers have this punishment power. They will engage in a myriad of options to forge meaning-ful relationships that ensure that sales keep coming. They will take the 66 or 166 raw data items from a customer profile and overlay as many maturation grids, value-processing modes, and adoption sequence models (see Chapter 3 and page 75, Chapter 5) as a marketing and sales department can turn out if it will help them do a better job of tapping into the value system of just one customer.

It is worth noting here that there are many sales positions where most or all sales calls are cold calls. In the absence of personal customer profiles, the profes-sional salesperson must match up the product to be sold with the various customer paradigms described in the previous chapter, so he or she can quickly identify the customer whose needs the product fulfills. Unlike someone who makes repeated calls on the same customer, the salesperson in this situation has but a few minutes to gain the potential customer's trust. For the salesperson faced with the need to reassure the cold-call customer, Joe Girard, a sales hero whose successes are recorded in *The Guinness Book of World Records*, has this sage advice: "Think about the fear you have sometimes felt when you want to buy some-thing. Then you can begin to understand what is going on in your customer's head when you meet him. Think of how people look for a friend when they are scared, and then be that friend."

Getting to know how your customer's mind works is a result of those face-to-face encounters during which the salesperson approaches the customer as a unique person. By being sensitive to the highly personal nature of the selling interface, the good salesperson quickly picks up on the nuances of the customer's personality and value system. As noted earlier, the customer's value system shapes the way he or she thinks, feels, and acts. It is the source of those emotion-driven attitudes that predispose them to act in a certain way — to buy. Getting close enough to the customer to gain this knowledge comes at a price to the salesperson. It means giving up a part of self, inviting others to view one as one views one's self. This willingness to become involved with another person is the hallmark of Rollo May's term, "social courage."

The Open Secret

"It is the courage to relate to other human beings, the capacity to risk one's self in the hope of achieving meaningful intimacy. It is the courage to invest one's self over a period of time in a relationship that will demand increasing openness," says May. While the relationships formed in selling are not usually the intimate, personal interaction of friends, they are nonetheless quality relationships. Often, they last a long time and are made up of people seen on a regular basis. The element of personal risk is worth a good working relationship; social courage is every sales hero's open secret. He or she will tell you this type of courage is an acquired trait that becomes second-nature with practice. It is the practice of caring empathetically. The ethical salesperson knows perfection of this acquired trait confers a certain power over others. He or she studiously avoids crass manipulation of others because she or he genuinely likes and respects people and has a true concern with helping them fulfill their needs. This is the natural self-discipline of caring.

Once acquired, this habit of social courage enables the salesperson to accept others as they are. It also allows others to accept the salesperson as he or she is. Exercising social courage helps conquer fear of the unknown by allowing the salesperson to go beyond the security and comfort of a narrow coterie of "business friends." Thus the salesperson is freed to get to know and like a host of additional people, and to assess and identify with their personalities and behaviors, their interests, and attitudes as well as their problems. In truth, the excitement of building relationships is in the very process itself: getting to know, like, and trust people in and for themselves.

Beating the Enemy Within

"Sounds easy," you might say. "But it's difficult to believe that a person can go from being a sales wimp to a 'Popeye' just by wishing it. Where's the spinach?" A good question. Ideas are changed, not by wishes, but by other ideas. New ideas knock out old ideas with their intensity. Changing a person's mind is a process of psychological surgery. We replace old ideas with new, more intense ideas.

In an earlier chapter, I suggested that the mind, like the body, is a living organism that must be fed good thoughts to ensure its health. To the extent we are our thoughts, sub-par thoughts are the enemy within. They can destroy us and our careers. Successful salespeople know this. They think for themselves and accept responsibility for their thoughts and the emotions and behaviors that follow from those thoughts. In their dealings with people, they avoid the dogmatic, close-minded thinking that leads to stereotyping, which can lead to prejudice. They are willing to do this even if it means unloading value-laden "baggage" based on their own socio-economic or religious backgrounds. They forgive all those who are not like them because they know and believe that there is nothing to forgive.

They do this consciously, knowing full well that it cannot be faked. In the words of C. S. Lewis, they treat all with whom they come into contact as "fellow immortals." The salesperson who accepts the way people look, think, behave, and process value in this spirit is sure to discover many likable and enjoyable qualities about them. Accepting diversity regardless of race, creed, class, or gender extends to any potential marker for prejudice — looks, political persuasion, age, or sexual orientation. Acceptance is one of mankind's deepest needs. When the customer feels the salesperson's acceptance, her or his natural tendency is to respond in kind. The salesperson who accepts diversity is a better person and a more functional human being.

Giving More Than You Get

The salesperson who welcomes diversity among customers is in a position to form lasting relationships based on mutual respect and trust. Such trust relationships have a positive influence on sales. As sales hero Joe Girard notes, "Make yourself a friend that your customer can trust and believe in. . . . If you are doing your job, you really do become that customer's friend.

I don't mean that you bowl with him or invite him to your house. Not that kind of friend. But the kind that a person can trust to treat him fairly and decently."

This is not as self-serving or insensitive as it might appear, although a surprising number of sales-people unwittingly buy into the stereotypical notion that selling is a deviously manipulative behavior and therefore tainted. Not true, for a number of reasons. The objective of the selling interface is not to make the customer so dependent on the salesperson that he or she can be led blindly into making a purchase decision that may or may not be in his or her best interests. On the contrary, the ethical salesperson is super-sensitive to the customer's needs and looks on the relationship as a partnership with shared respon-sibility for the buying decision: "I want my way for your benefit." He or she knows the only good sale is one that is a win-win for the customer, the sales-person, and the company.

Further, the customer knows the salesperson is there to sell her or his wares and accepts that fact. Consciously or unconsciously, from day one, the cus-tomer searches to determine whether or not this salesperson is worth knowing and trusting: "Will this person walk away from a sale if it is against my better interests?" Trust relationships are a substantial phe-nomena. The depth and richness of their develop-ment rests with the salesperson. The salesperson must demonstrate genuine concern for the cus-tomer's interests; must show that he or she is tuned into the customer's feeling and needs; and can be depended on to fulfill these esteem and peace of mind needs. From the initial call, the salesperson is out to establish credibility and trustworthiness to the wary customer — wary because most customers feel that the average salesperson couldn't care less about their real needs. To do this requires a positive attitude towards professional selling and a high degree of selflessness on the part of the salesperson.

The professional salesperson is a selfless individual whose focus is centered on the customer and away from self. This paradox comforts, given the undeserved "devious manipulator" rap on the selling profession. By definition, the salesperson is someone who wants things her or his way. What isn't so obvious to the critics is that good salespersons are willing to turn themselves "inside-out" to establish lasting relationships with those whose needs they wish to fill. The mentality of giving more than you get usually results in actually getting more than you give.

Achieving Hero Status

To gain the customer's trust, the good salesperson is open and frank about her or his intentions. Intentions are from the heart. Honest disclosure of the salesperson's thoughts and feelings will allay any customer suspicions that the salesperson is interested only in her or his own welfare. While the extent of this sharing of self will differ depending on the customer and circumstances, the emotional or feeling skills used to project the salesperson's true intentions are constant on every call. The feeling skills are worth enumeration and individual consideration, to wit: sincerity, empathy, humility, credibility, kindness, and tact.

The acquisition and projection of these skills are necessary to achieve hero status in a sales career.

Like courage, the constant practice of these skills results in perfected habits that make it difficult to act in any other way. Amish people practice honesty to the point it becomes a natural virtue. Dishonesty is not an option. Try putting your toothbrush in a different place every day. Sales heroes make relationship-building look easy because being sincere, kind, and tactful has become second-nature to them.

Again, these are acquired traits. No one is born with them. They are developed and taught primarily by role models. Anyone can develop and use them. This explains why sales heroes come with such diverse personalities and backgrounds, why their universal slogan is, "If I can do it, anyone can." Let's examine each of these feeling skills necessary for great success in selling.

Sincerity

Sincerity is a fundamental characteristic of the good salesperson. The sincere person is an earnest, tell-it-like-it-is individual whose style and speech truly reflect her or his thoughts and intentions. Sincerity is closely related to honesty and integrity. As an honest person, the sincere salesperson is not out to defraud anyone; as a person of integrity, the sincere salesperson can be trusted to put the interest of the customer above her or his own purely personal interests in the buying decision. Any salesperson who lives by this code will never want for customers. Customers will always know how serious such a salesperson is about the trust placed in her or him and how seriously the salesperson regards their business. The good salesperson's projection of sincerity is genuine. Such a salesperson can be wrong but never insincere. It is from within the person, and should in no way be confused with sudden, artificial smiles or puffed-up, evangelical enthusiasm for the product. It is never obscured by shallow, glad-handed, back-slapping superficiality.

Sincerity can be polished and perfected with practice, and it does carry over into the presentation of the product, inasmuch as the customer believes that the sincere salesperson has a good sense of what is important to know about the product. The salesperson has the belief and conviction that what he or she is saying and selling is the real truth of the matter.

Empathy
Empathy comes from the Greek words meaning "to suffer with;" colloquially we say we "walk in the other person's shoes." It is the capacity for feeling the projections of someone else as well as the ability to project one's own feelings into another human being. Empathy is critical to relationship-building. The salesperson, as empathetic listener, sensitively and non-judgmentally makes the customer aware that he or she understands the customer's feeling and meaning: "I desire to see the world as you do, and, in fact, I do." Be it an objection to a product claim or a formal product complaint, the empathetic salesperson reflexively lets the customer know that he or she knows where the customer is coming from.

Take the case of the pharmaceutical salesperson who approaches a key physician with a new anti-anxiety agent. At the mention of the product's indication, the physician pounds his fist on the desk and shouts, "I don't treat any anxious patients; I don't believe in the therapy. We're creating a drug-crutch culture and adults who take these agents are a bigger problem than the kids taking crack."

The salesperson's temptation here is to confront the customer head-on: "Yes but, doctor, you will admit surely there are many people who sometimes need this type of agent." Wrong. An empathetic approach is about the only hope this dialogue has of getting back on track: "Well you're right, doctor. Thank you for being so candid. There's definitely a lot of abuse. I can understand how difficult a choice you must have at times deciding who can really be helped by these agents. I'll tell you one thing, I certainly would not want to think of myself or my company as being a part of something that causes you difficulty." Empathy can change the direction of the dialogue.

Expressions of empathy may range from simple rephrasing what the customer says to adopting some of the customer's facial expressions or physical postures. Empathy is listening to and responding to feelings and sharing affects, an honest and convincing way to show concern. The customer trusts the empathetic salesperson because of a strong belief that the salesperson understands her or his needs.

Humility
Humility best defines the selfless nature of the sales professional. In this context, humble does not connote low self-esteem or a Uriah Heep–like submissiveness to gain the sale. Nor does it mean shy or introverted. Rather, it is a humility characterized by a

lack of arrogance or puffed-up sense of one's own importance. This humility manifests itself as courtesy, friendliness, and respect for the customer. It projects a clear message: "I am not here to impose my will on you or to act as your instructor. I am here to learn from you; to accept you and understand your needs . . . and, if possible, to help." Contrast this approach with that of the hypothetical salesperson who said in an earlier chapter, "I know you and what it takes to make you happy. Just listen to me and I'll make a believer and a buyer out of you."

Obviously, the customer who feels that he or she is held in high regard will be more comfortable and more amenable to the sale than the customer held captive by Colonel Blimp. The consideration shown towards the customer by the respectful salesperson comes from a genuine desire to build a close relationship and not from a vested interest to secure a quick sale. Humility is a critical skill in gaining acceptance from another human being.

Credibility

Credibility is the power or ability to inspire belief. Webster defines it from the customer's point of view as "assured reliance on the character, ability, strength, or trust of someone." The projection of credibility is one of the most influential traits that a salesperson can possess. Yet, like beauty, credibility is in the eye of the beholder; it is the customer's perception of the salesperson's believability. Many an honest, decent salesperson fails to project credibility because he or she ignores the first rule of motivational selling: Be yourself always and allow the customer to know who you are and where you are coming from.

As noted earlier, acting naturally rather than playing a role inspires in customers a special kind of trust and connectedness. People accept new ideas from those whom they know and trust.

Consider the following scenario, a version of which plays out in far too many sales encounters. A very presentable salesperson enters a customer's inner sanctum. For about 30 seconds or so, a person-to-person exchange of smiles and pleasantries takes place. Abruptly, the salesperson launches into the presentation, "Mr. Retailer, today I would like to introduce you to a new, distinctly different product: XYZ, blah, blah." The salesperson has assumed the role of monotone presenter while the customer becomes a bored listener. Why the transition from lively, bright person to automaton? What does this do for the credibility of the message as well as the messenger? The customer will never get to know, much less trust, a salesperson who repeatedly presents in this fashion. The disembodied presentation separates the sales message from the salesperson thereby draining it of credibility, since the customer recognizes it as a memorized product eulogy.

There should never be a transition away from the personhoods of both seller and buyer. The actions and words of the sales dialogue should retain the personal spirit and meter of the initial greeting.

If knowing the customer and letting the customer know you is step one in narrowing the credibility gap, a very close second is the customer's need for assurance that the salesperson has a thorough knowledge of her or his product and its applications. The customer depends on the salesperson's expertise for cogent reasons why her or his product fulfills the customer's needs. Sound product knowledge, which enables the salesperson to talk solutions in a way that makes sense to the customer, is a must for confidence-building. Product knowledge is a moral imperative for every professional salesperson and no amount of emotional intensity can substitute for it. How product knowledge is best utilized is the subject of a subsequent chapter.

To progress from a position of low credibility to the point of trust takes some doing, and during that "doing," the salesperson's dependability and trustworthiness are tested constantly. The salesperson must deliver consistently on promises made, as promised.

A word on this point: as promised. The smart salesperson does not go in for overkill or hyperbole in presenting product benefits to the customer. Product benefits should be carefully matched with those customer needs that they both recognize. Possible or potential additional benefits over and above those required to satisfy the agreed upon need are best left for later discovery or mutual discovery when attempting to extend product applications. Oversell means lack of sincerity, which drains credibility. Credibility is between undersell and oversell and ensures initial trial of product and a good shot at building a relationship. No disappointment is so acute as that experienced when we feel we have been let down by someone whom we trusted. Even if the perception is false, it can potentially destroy the relationship.

Kindness

Kindness may be the most revealing of the virtues necessary for successful personal interactions. Kindness is the projection of warmth, humanness, and genuine interest in another's welfare. Kindness is a quality that everyone can possess. Kindness is manifested as a tone — including tone of voice, mood, caring, consideration, and acceptance. It shines forth in voice, face, and attitude towards the customer. Kindness is something that everyone is pleased to receive. Good salespersons are nice people and are readily identified as such by their customers.

They know that by satisfying their customer's needs they will satisfy their own; still, they get a thrill out of the good feeling that comes with helping a customer fulfill a real need. They delight in the customer's win and in their own. The customer feels this good will and interest and, with each added win, places additional trust in such a person. Kindness is a positive quality in a person's makeup that enables that person to deal with difficult customers as well as those whom they might not like personally. Kindness is cool under pressure and can often defuse potentially explosive situations by calming the distraught customer with courtesy and good manners. In sales, contrary to the late Leo Durocher's lament, nice guys *do* finish first.

Tact

Tact is a keen sense of knowing what to do or say in order to maintain good relations with customers without giving offense; sometimes tact means saying hard things softly — in as kind a way as possible. It means having a clear perception of the best way to deal with the values and self-esteem of others.

Underlying tact is a certain prudence or practical wisdom that directs all the emotional or feeling skills under discussion. Tact ensures that none of these skills takes on caricature-like proportions that could work to the detriment of the salesperson. It knows the fitness of things. Tact recognizes space and turf. Tact dictates when to pull back in efforts to acquire better face-to-face knowledge of the customer; it senses when and where to cut off self-disclosure; and it avoids the temptation to shift blame to one's company when a little extra effort could clear up a customer's complaint. In sum, tact assembles all the feeling skills into a smoothly functioning sales personality that will carry that person to her or his goal: the making of a successful, superior salesperson.

The Core of the Soul of Selling

The salesperson's personality is an integral and essential part of the sales message. Make no mistake about it: Selling is a message because it is an emotional, practical art. When practiced as such, using all the feeling skills to project personality, it will produce the desired results: long-term relationships and impressive sales sheets. If you, as a salesperson, are sincere, empathetic, humble, credible, kind, and tactful and can project these qualities, you can be successful beyond your wildest imaginings. These principles constitute the soul of selling. You do not have to be a genius to understand them, nor a saint to practice them successfully. There are very few customers, no matter how hard-hearted or dogmatic they may be, who can resist the individual efforts of such a sales professional.

5. *The Call Itself*

Athletes and actors — let actors stand for the set of performing artists — share much. They share the need to make gesture as fluid and economical as possible, to make out of a welter of choices the single, precisely right one. They share the need for thousands of hours of practice in order to train the body to become the perfect, instinctive instrument to express. Both athlete and actor, out of that congeries of emotion, choice, strategy, knowledge of the terrain . . . must be able to change the self so successfully that it changes us.

A. Bartlett Giamatti

The sales call, like a play, is made up of actions and words; properly planned and executed, it invariably results in a happy ending. Like the drama, it has progressive scenes and acts, and the customer is invited to enter and join the progression as a full partner and participant. In fact, the customer becomes the star attraction without taking control of the action. The happy ending occurs when both the customer's utilitarian need for the product or service and his or her emotional needs surrounding the sale are fully satisfied. Product-oriented salespeople and sales managers, focused only on the sale itself and the signed order form, find this difficult to understand. They firmly believe the decision to purchase results from a logical exchange of verbiage centered on tangible features, advantages, and benefits of the product. For this group, animated, closely reasoned delivery of the sales message takes precedence over the customer's emotional needs.

Going for the Real and Lasting Sale

Do such presentations ever produce sales? Certainly. Are they "happy ending" sales? Not for all those customers whose needs aren't fully satisfied . . . and pity the poor product-oriented salesperson who spends a career attempting to deal with people in a non-human, artificial way (they call it sticking to business).

The motivational salesperson, on the other hand, knows the real and lasting sale occurs when the investment of feeling and emotion surrounding the product is meaningful beyond just the utilitarian need fulfilled. In fact, customers usually know their utilitarian needs. Some may know exactly how they will satisfy such needs; highly publicized, breakthrough products in universal demand may require only order-takers. Most buyers, even those who know their needs, require help when it comes to satisfying them. Buying decisions are stark risk choices and we

all desire help in making them rational. The salesperson spends his or her career with such buyers.

Emotional Linkage

Does the drama analogy, stressing as it does
emotion, suggest the ideal sales call "flies by the seat
of its pants" or "wings it" like Saturday night at the
Improv? Not at all. In fact, despite its call for personal
creativity and spontaneity, with no fixed recipes or
rules, the motivational sales call requires more care
and thought in preparation than any shortcut
"canned" presentation. The skilled performer/direc-
tor/salesperson with the courage to create plans it that
way. The salesperson is performer rather than actor
because everyone must perform to persuade; performing means being oneself to the fullest. As director, the salesperson draws on intelligence and imagi-
nation as poets and playwrights do in their endeavors.
The result may not compare to a poem or play in
artistic value, but it's a creative event nonetheless.

In pre-call planning each call, the skilled salesperson never loses sight of the individual when
applying any set of classifications. There are unique
aspects of every life and personality. Physical appearance, environmental circumstances, prized posses-
sions, casual comments, sensitivity to employees —
all are keys to buying needs and motives. For example, the self-esteem needs of the customer whose
diplomas going back to grammar school days cover
the walls are far different from those of the customer
whose office is tastefully decorated with excellent
reproductions of Dutch Masters. The salesperson
who has never thought to comment on a customer's
immaculately detailed, ten-year-old Porsche would

be hard-pressed to sell that customer a life jacket on a sinking ship. Selling is that simple and that complicated. Without emotional linkage with the customer, enhancement of self-esteem and subtle fear motivations are meaningless phrases.

Customizing the Call

Pre-call preparation enables the salesperson to set the stage for a successful sales call. It's a solitary exercise, but worth every minute spent since it results in a highly customized game plan for each call. This game plan will include all the activities the salesperson will engage in based on her or his knowledge of the customer. In the pre-call colloquy with self, the salesperson qualifies the customer in terms of utilitarian and personal needs as well as the salesperson's product and personality. Are they a good fit? If not, what can I do about it? What is my objective for this call? What are the best motivating factors for this customer? Where is this customer on the buying (learning) curve vis-a-vis my product?

Having worked out answers to these basic questions prior to the interview may not ensure smooth sailing on every call, but customers generally appreciate and respect the well-prepared salesperson. To attempt sales calls without having addressed these basic pre-call questions can invite disaster. Disaster in selling is always a "personal" matter. It is never a child of function alone.

Conceptual Models

Once the face-to-face assessment of the customer's value system is completed, the salesperson can verify and refine that evaluation using the various conceptual models discussed in Chapter 3. The maturation grid enables the salesperson to think about emotional selling approaches within the various age segments. Use of the value-processing modes gives the salesperson some ideas about connecting with client belief and value systems. Both these models help identify where the customer is in terms of product adoption. Easy to understand and apply, these mental models can help predict

FIGURE 4

	I Self-centered	II Self-esteemed	III Fair-minded	IV Self-actualized
Content (ages 65-beyond)			LM	
Creative (ages 41-65)	EA			T
Mature (ages 17-40)		EM		
Growth (birth to ages 15-16)				

| | Early
Adopters | | Early
Majority | | Late
Majority | | Traditionalists |

Column I represents a self-centered ("What's in it for me?") creative person (age 41–65) who is an early adopter (jumps on new products quickly).

Column II represents a self-esteemed ("Expand my horizon") mature person (age 17–40) who is an early majority (not first, but will try after usage grows).

Column III represents a fair-minded ("Is it balanced?") content person (age 65 and beyond) who is a late majority (will try only after others have tried).

Column IV represents a self-actualized ("Make me a more developed person") creative person (age 41–65) who is a traditionalist (will use only after widespread use).

behavior. For example, a salesperson would be foolish to attempt to sell a creative 55-year-old customer who processes value in the fair-minded mode ("Is it fair?") and who adopts products with the late majority on the basis of "new, innovative, breakthrough product," even if that customer has a real need for the product. Whereas to omit these same qualifiers when presenting the same product to the mature ("thirty-something"), early adopter who processes value in the self-centered or self-actualized modes would be a major mistake.

Some may think this type of categorical preparation for each sales call too mechanical or artificial. Not so. Better it be done in the salesperson's inner sanctum than in the customer's office at the expense of the sales interaction. It's the well-prepared salesperson who is in a position to improvise. Obviously, the models and modes we have so far developed are mere guides to how the customer may behave or react. They can be revised quickly as the sales dialogue unfolds. In fact, they allow for a more comfortable and relaxed dialogue since the salesperson who employs them is willing to go with the customer's flow instead of attempting to redirect the customer's psychological stream. The salesperson is usually seeking a relatively minor behavior change, not a psychological make-over of the customer. The use of conceptual models helps the smart salesperson control the process without needlessly jarring the customer's comfort zone. This is especially important when dealing with those customers whom the salesperson feels he or she does not match up well with because of temperament, socioeconomic background, or whatever. Being in tune with the customer's sociographics opens the way for the projection of the salesperson's feeling or emotional skills, which act to break down barriers.

Qualifying the Customer

Early in the pre-call planning process, the salesperson qualifies the customer in terms of both utilitarian need for the product or service and the ability to purchase. "Is my product helpful and practical for this person's business or life . . . Is it affordable?" Normally, this is not a complicated process, although it must be thought through for every call. Failure to complete this exercise for each call can result in wasted time, effort, and resources, not to mention dissatisfied customers stuck with unneeded products or services. It can mean the proverbial bad sale. In this context, it's worth noting that every time a responsible salesperson targets a customer for a product promotion and consequent sale, he or she, in effect, reaffirms his or her credo in that product or service's ability to fulfill that specific customer's needs. Anything less would be dishonest and could be ultimately self-defeating for the salesperson. Customers are quick to pick up on verbal or non-verbal signs that indicate a salesperson is not quite sold on the product. When this happens, customers feel hurt to be used this way and the salesperson's credibility suffers irreparable damage. Don't sell it if you're not sold. You cannot share what you do not possess! You cannot sell what you do not own!

The Call Objective

What do I want to achieve with this person on this call? Setting the call objective begins with the end in mind: What action do I want the customer to take as a result of my call? Whether the objective is to close a sale or to set up a future sale, it must be clear-cut and specific because it's what you seriously expect the customer to believe and do as a result of the call. Everything done or said contributes in a positive or negative way to the realization of the call objective.

Were the customer to say, "Fine, I'm sold. Tell me what you want me to do," the objective-oriented salesperson would be able to give that customer the "what, when, where, and how many" of the sale by chapter and verse on the spot. In the words of one stump philosopher I happen to know intimately, "The good salesperson always knows where to put the monkey."

Sadly, there's the flip side: The salesperson who arrives in the customer's inner sanctum without a call objective and, often, without any apparent reason for being there: "Thank you for being kind enough to see me, Almighty one. I know you are busy so I won't take up much of your valuable time. I don't really have anything new or very important. I just stopped by to see if you need to reorder product X and to see how you like it so far." Perhaps this is an extreme example to make my point, but it is the "substance" of many a sales pitch. Having heard many versions of this pitiful monologue over the years, I'm convinced that the original script was composed at some level of Dante's *Inferno*. Mediocrity is worse than bad in selling. It robs the salesperson of her or his dignity as a human being, steals away the customer's time (money) and defrauds the salesperson's company of the several hundred plus dollars it costs for each sales call. Not to mention the lost sales. Never make a sales call without a reason — without leaving behind a perception of value from the call.

Equally reprehensible is the take-the-cash-and-let-the-credit-go approach that puts making the immediate sale at any cost, even above the interests of both customer and company. This modus operandi ignores the fact that if either customer or company wins to the exclusion of the other, or neither wins in favor of the salesperson, it's a bad sale and one the salesperson is sure to regret. While everything done or said should contribute to the short-term objective of the sales call, never lose sight of the long-term objective that focuses on the complete picture of what you want to accomplish for and with this customer. Professional selling is working accounts, not just making calls. The objective of the sales call should be set in the context of a long-term mutually beneficial relationship.

Envisioning the Sales Call

Having completed the strategic aspects of the pre-call plan, that is, the evaluation of the customer's personality and value-processing modes, the identification of both utilitarian and personal needs for the product or service, and the establishing of the call objective, the salesperson is in a position to develop a mental picture of the tactics to be used during the sales call. While these tactics will vary from call to call depending on the strategic plan for the customer, they revolve around four factors essential for the success of any sales call: person, credibility, impact, and action. Collectively, they aim at securing emotional linkage with the customer from the beginning of the sales call through the moment of commitment to the sale and beyond. These four factors are customer-focused to ensure reality-based selling, and each is carefully planned prior to the call.

The Person Factor

Tactics based on the person factor are inspired by courage and willingness to be sincerely creative in human relationships. This personal approach can

FIGURE 5: **Sales Call Framework**

Alive Idea Component	Mechanical Objective	Human Objective
Personal Opening	To begin presentation and bridge to the alive idea.	To create customer comfort and a sense that the presentation is prepared exclusively for her/him.
Alive Idea	To focus on a product feature/advantage converted to benefit for customer.	To have customer realize that you have a mission. You must communicate your belief in the product.
Reinforcement/Proof	To visually reinforce with word and picture imagery your presentation focus (alive idea).	To create true credibility with customer by communicating that you and your company are trustworthy, that you do your homework.
Intensity	Use of example, illustration, success stories, demonstration, sample, etc.	To convey how much you and your company believe in the mission.
Close	Usually, to end the visit, motivating the customer to buy product or service based on your alive idea.	To communicate a sense of urgency and expectation for the customer to use a new approach. In other words — ACTION.

take the form of admiration, acceptance, interest, concern, or any of the numerous ways people signal a desire for rapport. The person factor must be tactful, sincere, and above all truthful, as most people resent forced or false praise. "Gee, what a beautiful desk you have here," doesn't cut it. Ideally, this personal factor should contain something unique to the customer that makes her or him feel as though this is the only call the salesperson is making that day. This happens when that something is directed to the personhood of the individual that may not relate to the product or business at hand, but has its foundation in the shared humanity of salesperson and client. Real pros avoid using a catch-phrase-of-the-day or joke-of-the-day approach, knowing that it's a psychological downer for a client to feel that he or she is getting the same staged treatment as a thousand other people. "What am I, chopped liver?" is the silent, if not expressed, refrain. The real pro addresses everyone as a person and is sensitive to that person's needs. Every customer is a territory.

The person factor tactic aims at acknowledging and complimenting the customer's humanness. However, the person factor can work both ways. As a sales manager, I once trained a young salesperson whom we'll call Mary, whose early career exemplified this factor.

Mary possessed all the required attributes of a good salesperson. But she was so nervous and anxious on her initial calls that her voice would shake and she actually would break out in red splotches around her chin and neck. The customers and I would share her distress; several asked if there was anything they could do to help since Mary's severe anxiety and nervousness were obviously related to the sales call. The blotches quickly disappeared after the call. Customers went out of their way to assist Mary and to make her feel comfortable. In fact, they dropped some of their own defenses to help her relax.

Admittedly, this is introducing the person factor into the selling dialogue in an elemental way. Mary's physical manifestation of her anxiety opened the door to a personal relationship with her customers. Customers were so preoccupied with making sure that Mary was okay that the selling situation was enhanced. With everyone, including Mary, striving to be more relaxed and less anxious about the business at hand, the person factor became the driver in Mary's initial sales success, since she was always cognizant of the sales situation. Today, without her shaking speech and splotches, Mary is a highly successful sales professional whose unruffled rapport with customers is the envy of both her colleagues and competitors. Clearly, it is incumbent upon every salesperson to find ways to relate to customers as human beings first and clients or customers second. The person factor is a cornerstone for long-term relationships.

No matter how aloof or imperious the customer may appear, the smart salesperson never forgets that he or she is dealing with a parent, grandparent, husband, wife, citizen, taxpayer, and a host of other roles that give rise to personal needs. As customers, people feel more at ease with the salesperson who inquires about one's family and its well-being, especially when there are indications over time that the interest is more than just a formality on the salesperson's part, i.e., remembering birthdays or graduations and the like year after year. On every sales call, the salesperson must execute something that is uniquely human directed to the personhood of the customer. The following are further examples of what might be called simple and complex ways the person factor plays out on a sales call.

The salesperson who related this first story to me was still somewhat amazed at the outcome. The salesperson had set up a project in an institution aimed at having her major product accepted by the institution on a rotating basis with the competition. Given the nature of her product and the industry, the project was both reasonable and doable. The institutional buyer, whom we will call Sonja, had other ideas. Sonja epitomized the fair-minded buyer;

she already had two products on rotation and saw no need for a third. She was adamant: no rotation, no change, no contacting other buying influences within the institution. This last prohibition went beyond her authority. Further evidence of her rigid policies: order day on Tuesdays only, no exceptions, and only in person.

Months passed and, despite headway with other buying influences, the salesperson began to feel the project was doomed. While working in the institution on a non-order day, the salesperson decided to pay the buyer a surprise visit with some new pricing information relating to several of her products in current use in the institution. The information would facilitate the proceedings of the following Tuesday's order day.

At the sight of the salesperson, the buyer became enraged. "What do you mean coming in here on a day other than Tuesday? Who do you think you are? You have no more right to be here today than someone passing by on the street outside!"

Stunned by this unexpected outburst, the salesperson managed to say, "Sonja, I'm very sorry. I stopped by to say hello to you and to ask you how you are. I heard you were ill last week."

Before the salesperson could say anything about the new pricing information, Sonja blurted out, "Ask me how I am on Tuesdays, not on Thursdays." Suddenly, as if realizing some hidden message in what she had just said, Sonja seemed to be on the verge of losing it. She turned and walked away. The salesperson left the pricing information with the buyer's assistant. Neither the salesperson nor Sonja referred to the incident again.

However, in subsequent weeks, the personal topic of Sonja's well-being and her dealings with a minor illness became the "person factor" that opened the door. Sonja's objections to the rotation project predictably began to fade. Within three months, the salesperson's product was on permanent rotation.

What happened? Who knows what was going on in Sonja's personal life on that day? Did she feel embarrassed on learning from the assistant that the salesperson had a legitimate personal reason for stopping by on a non-order day? Who knows? Certainly the timely delivery of pricing information had little to do with her change of heart towards the project. Certainly something of a personal nature occurred during that brief encounter. And order day is still on Tuesday.

My second example of the use of the person factor comes from my own experience. It demonstrates that the person factor is more than a superficial greeting or weather report; also, it illustrates the risk and vulnerability aspects of personal selling discussed throughout these pages. As a young but experienced pharmaceutical salesperson assigned to hospitals, I called on an eminent cardiologist who I'll call Dr. Hector, chief of medicine at a major teaching hospital. Dr. Hector enjoyed a national reputation as a consultant in his specialty; his word was law in the hospital. Rumor had it that, apart from his colleagues, Dr. Hector did not relate well to ordinary folk, least of all pharmaceutical sales representatives.

Rumor was right. During a sales call, Dr. Hector would appear very relaxed, one foot upon his desk and, surprising even for those times, smoking an ever-present pipe. He seemed distant and not very sociable; his responses to open questions were brief and dogmatic. Added to the frustration of calling on Dr. Hector was the pungent odor of his pipe, which permeated the office. A moment of truth occurred when Dr. Hector's approval was all that was required for formulary acceptance and hospital purchase of one of my company's products, which had several proven advantages over products then used by the hospital. Judging by his unresponsiveness to past appeals on behalf of the product, I was convinced that more of the same would fall on deaf ears. Dr. Hector just wasn't paying attention to me or anything I said.

I decided to use a person factor approach on Dr. Hector. After all, I reasoned, he willingly saw salespeople and, apart from being distant, was not otherwise hostile. Also, I knew he did not earn his lofty reputation by being a close-minded follower, so he might respect initiative in others.

With some trepidation, I opened my next call on Dr. Hector by saying right off in as playful and non-aggressive a tone of voice as I could muster, "Doctor, you don't know how much I dread calling on you." That got his attention because I was talking about him and he didn't know what was coming next.

"Well, why is that, Mr. Skinner?" he said. I'll never forget the generic way he said my last name, like it contained the names of everyone in the world.

"I start sweating the day I have an appointment with you," I continued. "Even the night before I begin to smell the damn smoke from your pipe. The memory is so real that I don't go into tobacco shops anymore. I used to enjoy an occasional cigar but I've given them up too, because every time I try one, I can smell your pipe. What's even worse, it reminds me of how you sit there and look through me like I'm absolutely nothing."

Dr. Hector smiled. Then he began to laugh and the laughter came from deep down in his chest. He wasn't embarrassed or angry and neither was I. In fact, this episode was the beginning of a long-term relationship that evolved into a lasting personal friendship. From then on, I made sure that every sales call on Dr. Hector began and ended on a personal note. He now had my permission to be a person. And I had his. Had I not acknowledged him as a person, he would still be the "perched cardiologist." Incidentally, the product proved its value to Dr. Hector's hospital and remains a standard therapy in hospitals throughout the country.

Reading this brief description of what, in reality, was a far more complicated personal interaction, some would say that the salesperson, despite playing off the pipe aroma and the doctor's aloofness in a lighthearted way, took a big chance, confronting the client with his own apparent insensitivity to others. Instead of being amused, Dr. Hector could have told me to stay out of his office if I didn't like the smell of his pipe. Agreed. Some risk existed.

However, keep in mind that the approach represented a carefully planned tactic. Tactics, as such, are highly individual and always open to second-guessing. The idea was to break down Dr. Hector's stereotype of me by focusing on an area of his vulnerability (his well-known aloofness and remoteness from people) while, at the same time, becoming vulnerable to his possible rejection or anger. It was his move. I was at his mercy. As I expected from many face-to-face encounters with him, Dr. Hector spared me, while demonstrating to himself that rumors of his coldness as a person were greatly exaggerated. An emotional linkage was initiated where previously none had been possible.

As Roger Ailes, adviser to U. S. presidents, notes, "Ironically, strength comes from vulnerability. This is true in public speech as well as interpersonal communications. . . . In business we're taught not to be vulnerable. . . . But imagine, as an alternative, that you toss a certain amount of your own vulnerability on the table. You're not frightened that you're going to be exposed or ruined or used unfairly. You choose instead to be open and candid."

Getting into the areas of each other's vulnerability is at the heart of the person factor in the selling interface. Unfortunately, average salespersons have a problem with the person factor. Not only do many salespersons buy into customer stereotypes of them; they actively promote their formation. They teach customers how to react to them and then must live with the stereotype. Predictable, almost stoic behavior on call after call patterns a customer into a habit of non-commitment. You must teach customers that you are a person! Otherwise, they label you a sales hack. A customer, accustomed to monotone presentations without meaningful personal interaction or dialogue, remains unimpressed or confused throughout the presentation of even a breakthrough product. How much easier for customer and salesperson if the person factor is part of every sales call. As a practitioner of the person factor, the sales hero is never weak-kneed at the possibility of failure or rejection on a call. He or she fears the fear but does the person factor on every call anyway. It's another example of social courage.

The Credibility Factor

What does the ability to project one's credibility do for the sales call and the salesperson? Ask the product directors for Advil® what Nolan Ryan's TV commercials do for their product's sales and their own careers. Ryan's obvious honesty and integrity, more than his remarkable baseball statistics, project a belief in the reliability of Advil that moderate pain sufferers find irresistible. By simply being himself and speaking in a conversational tone, he convinces thousands of viewers to try his product. His credibility as a person comes through to the extent that his low-keyed but intense testimonial, "Two Advil, and I'm ready to go another nine," ensures successful trial for a majority of Advil users. He epitomizes the credibility factor: He believes, therefore we believe. He is a solid, proven performer and, because of that, we believe his belief. He has a credibility factor.

Granted: the 30-second commercial is not a typical sales call, and there's only one Nolan Ryan. Actually, the sales call makes more demands on the salesperson's credibility than the TV spot, since the customer's perception of believability must be sustained and nurtured on every call and from call to call. Of all the feeling skills discussed in Chapter 4, the projection of credibility is the most influential trait any salesperson can possess. It qualifies you to help buyers make choices: Never forget it. On every sales call, no matter how complex, there must be something in the call that addresses the decency and honesty (that is, credibility) of the salesperson. It can be a subtle reminder of the extra mile the salesperson has gone for the customer in the past or the extent that the salesperson goes to get answers to customer questions.

Roger Ailes called the projection of credibility "using one's own natural life force," which he defines as "the energy we all have when we are interested in something and just being ourselves." Others sense the real you coming through. Les Brown, a popular motivational speaker seen on PBS, puts it more directly: "People buy because of your way of feeling. If you're not fired up, how do you expect anyone else to be fired up about it?" This trust-inspiring intensity or "life force" manifests itself in many ways: genuine liking and empathy for the customer; conscientious preparation for and follow-up on every call; thoroughness of product knowledge; and demonstrated reliability by delivering *as* promised *when* promised. The more change the highly credible salesperson asks for, the more he or she gets.

The Impact Factor

In the pre-call sales plan for each call, the salesperson must craft a doable impact factor aimed at creating a memorable impression on the client. In other words, create a memory. "What can I do or say that will make this customer proactive on behalf of my product?" is the question. How the answer to this question finds creative expression will determine the success of the call.

Given the noise level of the marketplace, the impact factor must be specific and unique. Most customers are exposed to hundreds of human and media contacts daily, all competing for their attention. If, as a salesperson, you are getting about 1/300th or so of that customer's daily media contact time to present yourself, your product, or your service, not to mention your opportunity to build a long-term relationship, your presentation must create an actionable memory in the client's value-processing system.

Ideally, the impact factor is designed around the presentation focus (features, advantages, benefits of the product or service) of the sales call and includes specific tactics for the use of pertinent sales aids. In effect, the salesperson plans the sights, sounds, and kinesthetics of the sales call beforehand, appealing to several senses to ensure maximum client interest and involvement. While it's a judgment call about where the emphasis goes on a given call based on the type of call being made, the salesperson knows that he or she must make any sales aid come alive with relevance to customer task and personal needs. An "alive idea," if you will.

On the other hand, unless incorporated into a unique personalized communication, the best sales aid in the world cannot sell a single product or service by itself. Used creatively, a good sales aid can be explosive; an otherwise harried and distracted customer can be made to sit up and take notice. Intelligently orchestrated, audio and visual sales aids can greatly enhance the kinesthetics of the sales presentation by enabling the salesperson to speak, move, and gesture in ways that reflect her or his confidence in the ability of the product or service to satisfy the customer's needs. How the impact factor is planned and executed is illustrated in the following case history from pharmaceutical selling.

In this case, the salesperson possesses a recent bulletin issued by the Centers for Disease Control (CDC), a prestigious government-supported agency based in Atlanta that monitors morbidity and mortality from all causes throughout the nation. The CDC regularly makes recommendations to the healthcare community based on its epidemiological findings. Once promulgated, these recommendations often become standard treatment procedures.

This particular bulletin suggests that staph infections, which hitherto have been confined mostly to hospital facilities, are increasingly being reported in community settings. Improperly treated staph infections can lead to serious illness. The CDC recommends that physicians who treat severe cuts, boils, and the like should consider the possibility of staph in all such cases.

The salesperson's company makes an anti-staph medication (Anti-Staph), which also kills most other common infection-causing organisms. The physician targeted for Anti-Staph promotion is Dr. Peters, a family practice physician, who is aware of the product but has used it infrequently because, as he says, "I don't see many staph infections in my practice."

While the impact factor possibilities for this CDC bulletin are obvious, it should be noted that physicians, in general, are not impressed easily on the basis of a single report. Otherwise, their prescribing habits would change on a daily basis. However, they do consider and weigh the source of new findings and recommendations. The CDC is a highly credible source. The report itself dovetails with the objective of the sales call: to motivate Dr. Peters to be more proactive in treating staph infections in his practice with Anti-Staph. The contents of the bulletin are relevant to Dr. Peter's practice and, presented with impact, should help the salesperson achieve this objective. Consider the impact value of two distinct approaches using the information contained in this bulletin:

Approach A: "Dr. Peters, you may or may not be aware of a recent bulletin from the CDC that states that staph infections are no longer confined to hospitals, but are being seen more frequently in community practices such as yours. The CDC bulletin suggests that physicians should be thinking staph when they treat severe cuts, boils, and the like. And Doctor, when you suspect staph, there are good reasons to consider Anti-Staph." This straightforward approach that may preface a general discussion of staph infections and Anti-Staph isn't bad; but its impact value is suspect, since it may not get the busy physician's attention.

Approach B: "Dr. Peters, I received a bulletin in the mail the other day from the CDC in Atlanta. I'm not sure I believe it. When you see a boil or a bad cut, do you ever think of staph infection?" Immediately, Dr. Peters is vulnerable. He must reveal what he does in his practice. He may say, "Generally, no," or "Why should I?" or even ask that the question be repeated if he hasn't been paying full attention. In any event, the salesperson gets to make a pertinent point to an attentive listener: "Dr. Peters, the CDC says that you need to consider every boil, every severe cut, and similar problem as a potential source of staph because the CDC's epidemiologic studies indicate that staph is widespread in the community. What it means is that in every situation where there is a potential for staph, it might be wise to add a sort of insurance policy. In places where you have been using our regular staph penicillin you really might consider using Anti-Staph."

The physician listens because it relates to something he does every day. By simply saying "I'm not sure I believe it," at the outset, the salesperson makes Dr. Peters the expert, thereby adding credibility to the dialogue. If Dr. Peters chooses not to believe it or act on it, it's his judgment against that of the CDC, not the salesperson, who is a mere conduit for the important information. In addition to the person and credibility factors, the salesperson introduces subtle fear into his impact approach. Interjecting staph infection into Dr. Peter's world where he doesn't normally look for it puts a strain on him. He must make a decision. Fortunately, relief is at hand: the solution is Anti-Staph. Despite the similarity of words used and the sharing of the CDC bulletin as a sales aid, the contrast between these two approaches in terms of the impact factor is striking. Approach A's sales call is recorded history. It's "in the books," to use an old baseball saying. Approach B's sales call created an actionable memory that continues to produce Anti-Staph sales.

Granted, the action factor or close is more than merely popping the question, "Will you buy my product, Ms./Mr. Customer?" Thus far, our examination of the soul of selling demonstrates that the selling process takes place within the framework of positive interpersonal relationships. The self-confident, courageous salesperson who prepares carefully for each call and who practices the feeling or emotional skills discussed earlier secures a series of commitments from the customer that lead naturally to a successful close. Throughout the sales dialogue, the salesperson seeks any number of minor and major commitments that indicate the extent of the customer's acceptance of both the salesperson and the product or service. Without dialogue, there can be no interim commitments. In such a case, the sales-person's plea for the order comes out of nowhere and falls on deaf ears. On the other hand, positive commitments fuel the selling process. They can be carried over and reaffirmed from call to call until the sale is closed.

While many of these action components cannot be planned prior to the call because they are generated by the dialogue, there are a number of techniques used by good closers to make it easier for the customer to buy. The skillful closer never puts the customer in a position that might prompt a sale-ending negative response: "Ms./Mr. Customer, don't you think my product deserves a trial?" or "Based on this advantage, will you use the product exclusively?" Parries such as these turn off a potential buyer.

In the first case, it's too easy for the customer to say, "No, I don't think it deserves a trial." That's the absolute end because the customer is now pre-pared to dig in and defend the decision against trial. The "Based on . . . will you?" is not totally unsuitable but may presume too much. The customer begins to think, "Whoa, wait a minute," and plans for a delay of sale.

The skillful closer uses non-threatening but intense phrases to help the customer paint a mental picture of the joy and satisfaction the benefits of the product or service will bring to his life. "Ms./Mr. Customer, with routine use of this product you are going to discover that your family . . ." or "You are going to find benefits you didn't expect . . ." The good closer creates an agreeable, friendly atmos-phere in which to ask for the order. The close must redeem the motivator.

The Action Factor

Ask for it. Ask for the customer's commitment to the product or service. That's the action factor of the sales call: what you desire to happen! Ask for it at the opportune moment, and continue to ask for it as often as it takes to close the sale. That's the job: To motivate others to do something specific on one's behalf. Asking can be critical to motivating.

Guess what? Most salespersons fail to ask for the order on the majority of sales calls they make. Many may think they do; they don't. Incredible, but true. That's why 20 percent of salespeople deliver 80 percent of the sales for most major companies. Think about it. Average salespeople, on the whole, spend their time setting the stage for their competitors, who get the business because they have mastered the art of asking for it.

Another quality of the professional closer is persistence. Of those salespersons who do manage to ask for the order, studies show that almost half give up after one "no," despite the fact that most sales are made after four refusals. If the product or service is right for the customer, the salesperson should never accept the rejection. Take it personally, yes, but never accept it as final. In saying "no," the customer exercises a human defense mechanism, and initial refusals are rarely final.

Rather, the rejection should be regarded as either a need for more information or a hitherto hidden objection. In either case, initial refusals should be welcomed as signals of customer interest. Rejection is a relationship bid. Beware of those who ignore you or who are neutral towards you. Love me or hate me, but never ignore me! When the salesperson

fully satisfies customer requests for added information or convincingly answers a customer objection, he
or she should ask for the order.

Such closing opportunities occur throughout
the sales dialogue. Though some may seem to be
minor commitment opportunities, they could has-
ten the final sale. After asking for the order, the
closer maintains eye contact with the customer and
goes silent until the customer responds. The closer
listens for the emotion in the customer's response
and, in the event of an additional objection,
responds to the emotion behind that objection.
Whereupon the closer again asks for the order and
silently waits for the customer to respond. If the
salesperson has truly motivated the customer
throughout the sales presentation, closing objections will be minor and "rationale-seeking" in
nature. In fact, at this point the salesperson would
be hard-pressed to stop the customer from buying.
Since "only them what asks, gets," the action component or close stands out as a critical component of
the four essential ingredients of the sales call. Still,
by definition, all four must be at work on each call
to ensure its success.

Earlier, we noted that the action factor or
close was more than simply asking for the order,
although many sales managers and selling manuals
would have you believe otherwise. Believe me: the
closing or call to action is more than a "yes" or "no"
check-off on a call evaluation sheet. Rather, it's a
process aimed at ensuring results; this process can be
helped along by a number of well-established closing techniques that go well beyond simply phrasing
a question. Let's look at some closing options:

Benefit Summary: The benefit summary close is particularly useful in situations where a number of small commitments or agreements on the benefits of the product have been made by the customer during the dialogue. The artful salesperson sums up these benefits in a series of one-liners that paint a good word picture with the customer squarely in the center, enjoying the self-esteem that comes from the benefits of the product and a decision well-made. With self-esteem through benefits, the customer feels like James Brown sings: "I feel good!"

Bargain Close: The bargain close works well in interpersonal selling because it extends the selling dialogue to the action itself. Its basic message is, "Ms./Mr. Customer, if I will do thus and so, will you do thus and so?" This quid pro quo approach is especially effective in closing with those customers who process value in the fair-minded mode ("an eye for an eye"). They see fair trades as a good way to conduct business. For the salesperson who recognizes this type of value-processing and who wants to participate in the action with the customer, the bargain close is particularly satisfying. The bargain close is very sound tactically since it all but guarantees customer action. It provides the tracks for the action to roll. The customer feels, "We're in this together."

Challenge Close: The challenge close is best employed in those situations where the salesperson must prove credibility to customers who may be committed to a competitive product (see section on the persuade call). Most people require proof to aid the purchase. This need for proof is especially acute where there is a high degree of resistance or objection towards you or your product. In such circumstances, the challenge close may be your only viable option. The approach is straightforward: "If I can prove that thus and so will happen to your benefit, will you do thus and so?" It employs elements of the bargain close with the added guarantee that the product, service, or salesperson will prove itself. It's a call to action through challenge.

Limiting Options Close: The limiting options close is especially useful where subtle fear is employed as the motivation. The principle behind the limiting options close is clear and concise. "Ms./Mr. Customer, if you want to enjoy this benefit, my product or service is the only place you can get it. This is your only choice if you want the peace of mind this benefit offers you."

Clearly, then, closing the sale successfully is more than just asking for the order. The call to action must be carefully orchestrated or induced out of the buyer's value-processing ego. Here is where the various conceptual models (maturation, value-processing, adopter sequencing) discussed in an earlier chapter can be helpful in analyzing the ego of the person with whom you are dealing. For example, people with powerful egos, justified or not, are often motivated by the slightest of reasons, almost by whim. They are difficult to motivate dramatically. Sales appeals based on enhancement of self-esteem do not generally impress such people, since they have more than enough self-esteem to go around. Yet, these same people often will be swayed by the subtle fear of missing out on the peace of mind delivered by some small, unassuming benefit of your product. It's almost as though they are above being

sold by the major, easily identifiable product benefits. On the other hand, the non-egocentric customers are motivated best by appeals that enhance
self-esteem. They need to hear the big, powerful,
dramatic reasons that enhance their self-worth and
elevate their self-esteem. The good salesperson
learns these principles early on and applies them in
ways that rarely fail to produce sales.

Meaningful Questions and Answers

In preparing the exposition or presentation phase of
the selling dialogue, the salesperson must determine
where the customer is on the buying (learning) curve
vis-a-vis the product or service. How familiar is John
Doe with your product's ability to fulfill his needs?
This includes personal as well as functional needs,
since it's John who must make the commitment.
Many an otherwise well-thought-out, mechanically
sound presentation falls into the "good presentation,
but no sale" category because it overlooks the customer's personhood in the planning stage. This holds
true whether the call is being planned for a potential
buyer or user buyer. Virtually all one-on-one sales
presentations fall into one of four types: introductory,
persuade, expand, and cultivate. Before examining
the four types of calls in depth, it's worthwhile con-
sidering two basic communication skills employed by
sales pros to gauge customer attitudes and emotions
in order to change behavior: productive questioning
and active listening. Your ability to ask attitudinal
questions and listen for the real meaning behind the
customer's response will determine the aliveness of
the feature/advantage/benefit dialogue that you conduct on each of the four types of call.

Productive Questioning

The productive question is a true question, prompted by a sincere desire to know the answer. It seeks a real answer that the salesperson needs to know to fulfill her or his responsibility to the client. Usually, the productive question is attitudinal in nature: it seeks to connect with the client's feelings and emotions. The true question is never self-serving and is easily distinguished from the timed probe or stop-on-the way-to-the-sale gimmick advocated by many of the "canned skills road maps." Such road maps suggest the use of the probe as a device to carry on the dialogue whether or not the salesperson wants to know the answer, or, even worse, when the salesperson already knows the answer to the question being asked. Such questioning tactics destroy the salesperson's credibility and violate the spirit of the emotional or feeling skills crucial to long-term relationship-building. Method acting may work on the stage, but there is no such thing as method selling.

Tactful questioning often begins the sales dialogue, keeps it going, and, as noted in the section on the action factor, is vital in securing the commitment to the sale. It ensures that the dialogue is a two-way interaction with wins for both buyer and seller. The customer gets involved and feels that her or his ideas and opinions are important to the salesperson, who, in turn, is able to align with those thoughts and feelings in such a way as to solve the customer's problems. Although there are probably as many types of questions as there are emotional adjectives, questions are generally described as open-ended or closed-ended.

To appreciate the difference between open- and closed-ended questions, think of the press-conference format. Reporters, seeking the broadest possible answers, ask open-ended questions that begin with words and phrases such as "what," "why," "could," "how," or "What do you think about . . . ?" and "How do you feel about . . . ?" When the person being interviewed gives an abrupt "yes" or "no" answer to an occasional closed-ended question, it often draws a laugh. Case closed: next question.

Although open- and closed-ended questions are employed throughout the selling dialogue, they are never used in the interrogatory way of the press conference. The client should never be put on the spot. While closed-ended questions aren't very helpful in moving the dialogue along, they are often useful in determining the course of the sales presentation, i.e. "Does your company still believe in EXES technology?" Sincere open-ended questions get the customer talking about her or his needs and wants. Such questions encourage the customer to elaborate on specific issues. When queried tactfully, even the most reticent of customers often will share their innermost feelings and opinions. They will discuss freely their dominant buying motives with the attentive salesperson. Still, it takes courage and confidence to enter into these two-way exchanges with customers.

Open-ended questions give the floor to the customer and the salesperson may not like what the client has to say. Weak salespeople give monologue sales presentations or make quickie door-knob sales calls because they fear loss of control or loss of face in such interactions. Real pros who control the selling interface don't feel frightened or threatened in such situations. They welcome dialogue knowing that favorable or unfavorable data supplied by the customer is the key to completing the sale successfully. Nor do they fear being asked a question that they don't have an immediate answer for. It just proves that they're fallible and the customer is perceptive. Also, getting the answer is part of their commitment to good service.

Skillful productive questioning aids in projecting the feeling or emotional skills such as empathy, sincerity, and humility. Plus, they introduce the person or credibility factors into the sales dialogue. Take empathy, for example: the sensitively asked question, "Ms./Mr. Customer, how do you manage to cope with this difficult area that requires so much of your time and effort?" communicates the questioner's desire and ability to see things from the customer's point of view. At the same time, it projects humility: "I don't know or presume to know everything about your situation. I am not your typical all-knowing, manipulative salesperson."

Skillful productive questioning projects sincerity because it studiously avoids predictable, stereotypical "sales-speak" language and behavior.

The first rule of the good salesperson is: Don't meet the customer's preconceived expectations of what you are going to say or do during the selling interview. In other words, violate their expectations. Why? Because those expectations before the sales call are so low that, by living up to them, you compromise your sincerity in their eyes. Not to mention your credibility. When we speak and act as expected, the selling interface is reduced to a strict, humdrum business proposition. Banality rules and there can be no impact factor.

How can the salesperson avoid stereotypical language and behavior? Begin by reshaping what you know to be the expected message. For example, the customer expects the salesperson to exaggerate the features, advantages, and benefits of the product. That's typical behavior. Suppose the salesperson were to say, "Ms./Mr. Customer, I do have one concern that you can possibly address. Does my product have any disadvantages from your perspective?" Suggesting the possibility of a disadvantage seems risky, but it goes a long way towards establishing the salesperson's sincerity and credibility because it breaks the mold of preconceived expectations. Productive questioning avoids stereotypical language and behavior. Good productive questioning focuses on the customer's real needs. To be productive, questions must be specific and directed to the customer's own needs and concerns. Avoid questions that give the impression of being preplanned as part of a selling tactic. Without doubt, the greatest use of productive questioning is the projection of the feeling or emotional skills.

Active Listening
The best professional salespeople are the best listeners. Their collective motto: Listen your way to the sale. They know that only by listening to the customer will they know what it is they want to change or create. They absolutely need the data. They put no credence in the conventional wisdom that holds that the salesperson should do most of the talking on a sales call. Sometimes, perhaps, in the case of the extremely reticent customer, but certainly not as a general rule. Most misunderstandings between buyer and seller are due to poor listening habits, and many salespeople fail in their selling careers because they don't take the time or make the effort to listen to

their customers. They bring their own inner distractions to the sales call; they pretend to listen to what the customer has to say while they are thinking only about what they are going to say. Often, the inattention is so obvious in facial expression and body language that the customer is forced to do a reality check: "Do you hear what I'm saying?" Sad, but true. "Listen attentively more than you speak" should be posted in capital letters on the visor of every salesperson's automobile. It's a key to success.

If the objective of productive questioning is to set up the best conditions for idea exchange, the main purpose of active listening is to search out the common ground on which the salesperson and customer can agree on how they feel about a product or service. Active listening leads to common understanding and mutual trust. It's the *sine qua non* of good rapport because the customer invariably responds in kind.

Effective, active listening is non-judgmental and empathetic. It is non-judgmental since the salesperson listener does not use personal or preconceived ideas to screen out things he or she doesn't agree with or doesn't want to hear. What the customer has to say doesn't need to fit the salesperson's pre-call conceptual plan; that is, many salespersons commonly ignore anything the customer has to say and deliver the sales message prepared for the call. Effective listening is empathetic. The active listener tunes in the speaker's real intent in order to understand and align with the values and attitudes behind the words. He or she listens for feelings as well as words.

To characterize active listening as non-judgmental and empathetic doesn't mean to imply that it is uncritical. Far from it. People don't always say what they mean or mean what they say; many times they'll tell you what you want to hear. Using all five senses as listening posts, the skillful communicator absorbs all the subtle clues intended to throw people off without ever knowing it — facial expressions, tone of voice, body language, and connotations of the words used. Subconscious messages given off by the client frequently convey the information the salesperson needs to change that customer's buying behavior.

The professional salesperson knows that everyone is strongly motivated to resolve the dissonant behavior they find within themselves — what they do versus what they say. When sales pros sense customer dissonance surrounding a product or service, they seize the opportunity to affect that customer in a way that changes her or his behavior. The appeal must be emotional at this juncture; logic won't do.

Faced with their own dissonant behavior, people tend to hear what they want to hear and proceed to act or buy as they did previously. Enter the active-listener salesperson, whose skill is to interject an unexpected fact with passion and resolve the customer's dissonance so that he or she feels compelled to change her or his attitude towards the product or service. As we shall see, this ability has special pertinence in conducting the persuade call where the decision has already been made against the salesperson.

Productive questioning and active listening on the part of both salesperson and, to a certain extent, the customer are at the heart of the sales communication cycle. They create the ideal milieu for seller and buyer to listen, value-process, and respond to each other as living, breathing human beings. The feedback they get from each other in such exchanges keeps them on the same wavelength and keeps the partnership on target for the sale.

Features/Advantages/Benefits

Verifying needs through productive questioning and active listening enables the salesperson to link product features and benefits with the customer's real task and personal needs. The old sales maxim says it all: "You can't sell a person until you know what he wants, but once you know what he wants, it's easy."

The salesperson creates value by demonstrating to the customer that the benefits of the product fulfill these needs in a unique or special way. The commitment comes when the customer accepts this value intellectually and emotionally. Like credibility, value is in the eye of the customer, despite how marvelous the salesperson may think the features and benefits of her or his product or service are. Enthusiasm and belief in one's product are essential components of the successful sales call; but getting too wrapped up in the presentation of feature and benefits for their own sake can kill the sale. Creating value around features and benefits means showing the customer what it will mean to her or him personally to own the product; how the product or service solves that customer's specific problem.

The feature/advantage/benefit triad forms the core of the verbal portion of the sales communication. Ideally, this information exchange takes place in a partnership atmosphere set up by the salesperson's adaptive behavior, such as the use of the emotional or feeling skills. Since the emphasis on feature/advantage/benefit varies with the type of call being made, the salesperson must have a clear understanding of what they mean and how they are used on the sales call.

Features: A feature is a characteristic or quality of a product or service that defines what it is, what it looks like, or what it does. It describes the product or service itself: non-sedative allergy formula, vacuum cleaner with built-in attachments, etc. These features in and of themselves have no value until related to customer needs.

Advantages: An advantage describes what the feature does in a unique or special way. Lacking the latter, the salesperson must reposition the product based on a feature/advantage story that competitors may share but are not promoting or, better yet, based on a need verified by the customer in dialogue.

Advantages are comparative and relative. The salesperson uses them to create value when matched to customer interests. Unlike other systemic allergy formulas, the non-sedative allergy preparation relieves symptoms without causing drowsiness; unlike most standard vacuum cleaners, the vacuum cleaner with built-in attachments enables the user to pick up dirt and dust on every object in the room. Unfortunately, many salespeople stop selling at this point in the mistaken belief that the customer sees the obvious benefits of the product for his or her own life. This is a big mistake in selling, not tying advantages to customer needs to realize a benefit for that customer. In the discussion of the action factor, you will recall the skillful closer always relates the advantages to the customer with phrases such as, "You will discover . . ." or "What this means to you . . . ."

Benefits: A benefit is the value of the product or service to the customer. It relates the features and advantages of the product to the customer's value-processing mode in order to dispose her or him to purchase the product or service. It answers the questions "So what?" or "What does it mean to me?" The non-sedative allergy drug enables the patient to function normally during allergy season. In addition, the prescribing physician derives a benefit each time a patient reports back, "Doctor, I don't know how to thank you . . . for the first time in my life . . . ." The one-stop vacuum cleaner is more convenient, saves time and, best of all perhaps, eliminates aggravating search for attachments on cleaning day.

In creating value for the customer, the skillful salesperson aids the buying decision by pointing out how much better off he or she will be as a result of acquiring the product or service. Mutual agreement on benefits goes a long way towards ensuring successful initial trial, as well as enhancing the salesperson's credibility.

How features/advantages/benefits are used in the context of the sales call will vary with the type of call: introductory, persuade, expand, cultivate. Most one-on-one sales calls fall into one of these categories, and it's essential that the salesperson shape the presentation accordingly, to ensure its buyer friendliness. Otherwise, the presentation focus of the call is unreal. If the salesperson doesn't know where the potential buyer is on the buying curve, he or she should ask, and then listen carefully to the response.

Introductory Call
Nothing is greater than communicating with another

human being, especially when the information shared involves the new and different. For the professional salesperson, it's a rare and exciting selling experience to introduce and motivate a customer to use a new product or service whose advanta es and benefits the customer might otherwise have missed. Since the presentation focus of the introductory call (see Figure 5, page 80) spotlights the features, advantages, and benefits of the new product or service, it's worth reviewing the various steps required to promote the new product or service within the framework of the sales call (see Figure 6).

FIGURE 6: Introductory Call

To present the new (rare and exciting)

When	• New product, new salesperson
	• New customer moves in
Objective	• Deliver presentation focus on basic product features/advantages/benefits (accenting a balance of the three)
	• Address anticipated sales issues
Impact	• Alive idea based on balanced features/advantages/benefits
Close	• Assure successful initial trial

Step one is the personal opening. Every selling manual agrees the formal objective of the opening is to build a bridge to the presentation focus or selling proposition. To do this successfully, the opening must achieve its human objective, which is to create a climate of customer comfort and a sense on the part of the customer that the presentation to follow was prepared exclusively for her or him. In a good opening, the salesperson aligns with the client's interests in a way that invites and encourages participation in the upcoming dialogue.

The opening should be prepared as carefully as one would prepare the opening words of a speech. It's critical to get off on the right foot. Too many salespeople rely on the inspiration of the moment to begin a sales call. Often what comes out leaves the customer wondering what happens to people when they go into sales. For example, "Mr. Day, I'd like to take a few minutes of your time to tell you about something new and wonderful that my company has developed. I know you are busy, but it won't take long and you may be interested." As versions of these trite phrases are spoken, most potential customers go back to thinking about their main preoccupation of the moment.

Contrast this with the personal tone of the following opening: "Mr. Day, when I was preparing for work today, I thought of you. I thought about a discussion we had some time ago. I could see your face and I distinctly remember your description of what you felt would be an ideal product for your business. Well, I'm happy to tell you that my company has just released such a product and I wanted you to be among the first to know about it." It's simple and not contrived since it's based on a shared experience. The customer at once knows why the salesperson is there and looks forward to participating in the dialogue because he is reminded of his existing interest.

The introductory call opening has some pitfalls in and of itself. In the enthusiasm of the moment, the salesperson may jump right into presenting features and benefits without aligning with the customer's interests. When this happens, the customer feels left out. The opening that ignores the personhood of the customer has about as much chance of resulting in a sale as the new salesperson who, after a patently egocentric self-introduction, says in effect, "Try me, you'll like me." No thanks, every time.

Having gained the customer's attention and interest, the salesperson proceeds to reaffirm the customer's personal and task needs through tactful questioning and active listening. This is especially true when introducing a new product whose major features may result in several benefits with priority ratings that differ from customer to customer. For example, the buyer with a slight build may be more interested in the size and weight of the one-stop vacuum cleaner as compared to conventional units before any discussion of the more obvious convenience and time-saving benefits. Specific needs must be established and agreed upon before a relevant feature advantage/benefit package can be shaped.

The best presentation cannot make up for the lack of a good basic selling idea, an idea that comes alive because it is humanized by the salesperson for a specific customer. This is reality-based selling. The introductory information package for a new product may be a cornucopia of new features, advantages, and benefits, but it's the salesperson who must tailor these features and benefits to the customer's value-processing system to show how they are superior to the product or service in current use. The salesperson selects those features whose advantages and benefits he or she knows the customer will value highly, while communicating the sincere belief that the client will enjoy and be delighted by the superior results. In the introductory call, the action word is the unspoken "try" and the impact factor is built around features, advantages, and benefits.

Proof materials offered in support of superiority claims are often the key to success in this type of call. The credibility of both salesperson and company hinges on how well this is accomplished. In the case of the vacuum cleaner, demonstrate the unit under real conditions. Or, better yet, have the potential buyer operate the machine. This should reinforce the all-in-one benefit/advantage claims. In introducing the physician to a new systemic allergy medication with non-sedative properties, the salesperson must present strong and convincing proof because the concept goes against the grain of the physician's education and experience. For example, double-blind crossover studies published in reputable journals with peer review are essential in this situation. Such proof materials indicate the company does its homework and is not out to promote unsubstantiated claims for its new products.

Dialogue can occur anytime throughout the presentation focus and reinforcement/proof phase of the introductory call. Customer queries and objections are welcomed as opportunities for trial closes that will make the final close that much easier. Such dialogue enables the salesperson to demonstrate the intensity of his or her belief that the product or service will do what he or she says it will do for the customer, for example, by relating success stories based on experiences of satisfied customers and use of other demonstration materials. The action or close of the introductory call aims at ensuring positive trial of the product or service by summarizing only those features/advantages/ benefits of the new product that buyer and seller have agreed will satisfy the customer's current needs. This agreement will go a long way towards ensuring successful trial since the customer's expectations will center on those agreed upon in the summary benefits dialogue.

Persuade Call

The objective of the persuade call (see Figure 7) is to switch the customer from a competitive product or service with which he or she is satisfied to the salesperson's own brand. It is the most difficult and most challenging type of call in the salesperson's repertoire, and the most frequent. Its importance varies with the amount of business involved. Consistent success in making the persuade call is the mark of the master salesperson. To win the day on any persuade call requires intelligent pre-call planning of the alive switching idea to be used, as well as a specific plan for each of the four factors based on the salesperson's knowledge of the customer. The action word is change and the impact factor will focus on the unique advantages and added benefits for the customer over and above the product in current use.

Granted, all selling is about change and seeks behavior modification. What makes the persuade call so difficult is that the customer has already made the decision against your product. It's not an even playing field; going in, the score is 100 to 0. The fact that it was the customer's decision in the first place almost ensures brand loyalty. The customer will feel, "It's doing the job," even if not deliriously happy with it. He or she will think, "My decision was a good one."

FIGURE 7: **Persuade Call**

To initiate change

- Most frequent type
- Challenge to a salesperson
- Knowledge, skill, and planning critical

When	• Competitive product being used
	• Resistance to change
	• Objection use

Objective	• To switch customer from competitive product

Impact	• Alive "switching" idea based on product's distinctive advantage

Close	• Close on exclusive benefits
	• Consistent follow-up

The suggestion or thought of change, especially an about-face type of change, produces anxiety and the fear of risk in the satisfied customer: "You're in my wheelhouse, and I don't particularly like it."

Often such a customer will simply tune-out any benefit/solution recitation by the salesperson because he or she doesn't want to face the consequences of change. Change is an emotional procedure. This is especially true in buying and selling products and services. We know what we like and like what we know. We resist even small changes. When was the last time you changed toothpastes? As discussed in the chapter on enhancement of self-esteem and subtle fear motivators, we buy more from feelings than facts, otherwise we all would be wearing dollar watches and generic shoes. From the personal opening to the close on exclusive benefits, the persuade call requires full use of the emotion or feeling skills. People change for people. Logical reasons are rarely the motivating factors behind behavioral change. This is more than the salesperson's credo; it's human nature.

What does it take to carry out a successful persuade call? Once you are convinced that the switching idea offers product or service benefits that the customer is not getting from the one in use, you must have the courage to engage the client in exploring the reasons why the negative decision was made. During this interaction, let the client do most of the talking. Your role is that of empathetic listener. Listen, listen, listen — that's the key to setting up the switching idea in the presentation focus. The customer will tell you what he or she needs to hear about your product. By active listening, you align with the customer's feelings and emotions prior to changing attitudes and opinions. In classic sales jargon it's called "going down the road . . . but."

No matter how outlandish the objection or bias against his or her product, the skillful pro agrees with the client up to a point, whereupon he or she tactfully attempts to set the record straight. "I felt exactly the same way as you do up until last week when one of my customers shared her experience with me . . . ." Through a series of empathetic responses, the salesperson begins the process of deprogramming the customer's negative attitudes towards the product or service. Customer responses throughout the deprogramming phase will indicate how much he or she is listening. It's crucial that the customer listen. Only when the brand-lazy customer is made to feel uncertain or uncomfortable with her or his current position will the added gain of the switching idea be heard and recognized to the point of "Well, I've got to try that."

Sounds easy, but it's not. Clothing the switching idea in one or both of the enhancement of self-esteem or subtle fear motivators calls for creative, on-the-spot thinking and bold action. Despite the deprogramming efforts, the customer has opted for the competitor's product and could remain very defensive or even hostile. In such situations, many salespeople feel the stress and allow themselves to be intimidated.

The key to the successful persuade call is emotional control of the selling process. At some critical point, the salesperson must challenge the customer to take advantage of her or his product's superior benefits. Ideally, this critical point occurs in a moment of customer uncertainty about the product in use; at this point, perhaps unexpectedly for the customer, the salesperson spells out the personal gain the customer can realize if he or she makes the switch.

The confidence, and to some degree the courage, to make the persuade call arises out of the distinct advantages of the salesperson's product that separate it from the customer's current choice. It's good for the customer. Although not so stated, the spirit of the persuade call is, "My product is far better for you than the one you are using." It's comparative all the way. The presentation focus is on how much better off you will be when you make the change. It asks for commitment on the basis of exclusive benefits as demonstrated by visual aids and supported by proof materials.

When closed on a positive comparative note, the persuade call provides plenty of emotional space for the customer to feel comfortable and safe with the decision to change. The real pro lives up to the old Sears Roebuck motto "Be easy to buy from." He or she stimulates the client to change but also gives that client the opportunity to do it in her or his own way so there is no loss of self-esteem. The customer just made another, better decision.

Expand Call

The expand call (see Figure 8) aims to create new business from an already satisfied customer by motivating her or him to expand product usage into new areas of application. This type of call has several things going for it: the change asked for is usually not radical; as a satisfied user, the customer already has a positive emotional investment in the product or service; and the credibility of the salesperson and her or his company are well established in the customer's mind. Rapport exists. As a salesperson, you are in a good spot because conflict is usually minimal. Still, you can't be complacent because the expand call requires creative pre-call planning all its own. This is especially true when the area you are looking to

FIGURE 8: **Expand Call**

To create new business for satisfied user

| When | • Customer comfortable with the product |
| | • Currently using but not to full advantage |

| Objective | • Build on present base |
| | • Transfer benefits enjoyed in areas of customer comfort to desired expansion areas |

| Impact | • Alive idea focuses on features from which flow added advantages and benefits |

| Close | • Close in on new business by stressing benefits |

expand into with your product has been preempted by a competitive product. In this case, you are faced with making a combination persuade/expand call. Also, taking advantage of the benefits derived from different features of the same product may take some explaining, even when dealing with the most sophisticated of clients.

For example, the physician who takes advantage of the sedative features of an anti-anxiety drug in his surgical practice may be reluctant to use that same anti-anxiety agent in his ambulatory patients who must function normally during the day. He understands the logic but he would just as soon use a different anti-anxiety preparation to be on the safe side. A competitor's subtle fear phrase? A very strong possibility. At any rate, logic and emotion are in conflict within the same person, and it's the salesperson who must step in and impact with a non-sedating, lower dose feature/benefit story that overcomes the client's current emotional bias.

The expand call is about feature(s) and the added benefit(s) that will accrue to the customer who takes advantage of these newly perceived feature(s). That's the message and the impact of the presentation focus in the expand call. Highlight the features, what they are, and what they do that's different, and always provide good benefit resolution.

The close of the expand call is always specific in the action desired. Sometimes, not often, the customer will take it away from you and suggest the action. Building on the present usage base, the close can be paraphrased as follows: "You will be just as satisfied with the benefits derived from use in this new area of expansion as you are now with the benefits you enjoy in your current area of use. I implore you to look at this new and exciting area and the benefits that my product is capable of delivering. If you accept the new area of benefit, you will want to try the product in this specific expanded area of use." It's a limited option close used often in basic selling that is very effective.

Cultivate Call

The cultivate call (see Figure 9) aims at maintaining maximum product or service usage by the committed customer in the face of competition. Unlike selling situations that present one-time opportunities, the cultivate call presumes repeat visits on the same committed customer. The cultivate call is selling in the fullest sense since it takes place in the context of the long-term relationship. In fact, the modus operandi of the cultivate call is fully developed in the chapter on long-term relationships. You maintain your business by continuing to build on all those credible, empathetic, person things you did to get the business in the first place. Long after the sale is made, the real pro continues on every call to plan for and to address those reasons for the customer's purchase that were not related to the product itself, as well as those benefits currently delivered by the product.

Almost instinctively, the professional salesperson operates on the implicit truth of Pascal's observation, "The heart has its reasons which reason knows nothing of." The good salesperson never takes a hail-fellow-well-met, thank-you-very-much, see-ya-later approach towards a committed customer. Apart from the insensitivity manifest in such an attitude, the salesperson knows that competition is waiting in the wings with eye-popping switching strate-

FIGURE 9: **Cultivate Call**

To maintain maximum usage

When	• Now getting the business in most or all important areas
	• Danger in vulnerability from competition

Objective	• Verify current use
	• Make it easy to continue
	• Constantly reinforce benefits
	• Vaccinate against ravages of competition

Impact	• Alive idea focuses on features on summary of benefits and compliments on good decision

Close	• Express appreciation
	• Close in on continued maximum usage

gies ready to go at the first signs of customer uncertainty or salesperson neglect. We don't need studies to tell us that the vast majority of product switches occur after a certain period of benign neglect on the salesperson's part rather than dissatisfaction with the product or service involved. The tone of the cultivate call may be described as heart-to-heart (warm fuzzies) but the call itself takes nothing for granted and leaves nothing to chance. The cultivate call may be the most important of the sales calls.

The objectives of the cultivate call are fourfold: to verify current usage; to make it easy to continue using; to reinforce benefits; and to vaccinate against competition.

Due vigilance prompts the alert salesperson to seek periodic verification of usage. Productive questioning and active listening for any signs of dissonance in the responses of customers or others close to the sale will tell the salesperson where he or she stands. Reminders of reliable, dependable past service as well as ready availability when needed make it easy for the customer to continue use. As proof of that good service, the committed customer should be among the first on the list for expand calls, since you don't want her or him to learn of new product applications that could bring added satisfaction or profit from another source. Keep the committed customer fully informed to ensure continued use of your product, even if he or she rejects the expanded usage initially.

"Maintain usage" is the action phrase of the cultivate call; the impact of the presentation focus is on product benefits currently enjoyed (the "so what's" of the product's features and advantages). As promised, it continues to be a good solution. The alive idea summarizes all those good things that continue to flow from the decision to purchase. The cultivate call closes on a note of genuine appreciation for the business and an honest appeal for continued maximum usage. The customer is made to feel that her or his business is of major importance to the salesperson who is committed to leaving no stone unturned in efforts to service that customer to the fullest. When this is accomplished in the cultivate call, the salesperson, in effect, has vaccinated the committed customer against the potential ravages of the competitor's diseased switching idea. Business gained has been maintained.

Performer/Director

This chapter began with the suggestion that the sales call is somewhat like a play in which the salesperson is not only a live performer but also a director of the event. I say performer rather than actor since it's crucial to be one's emotional self in order to persuade. Reason alone doesn't work. Canned message presentations are almost impossible to carry out with credibility because the dynamic of the selling relationship does not lend itself to word-for-word scripting. The sales call is alive and interactive, which means there is no short-cut around the meticulous pre-call planning necessary to carry it off successfully.

David Lean, the late movie director extraordinaire, once remarked, "I have the negative in my mind: I try to make the positive happen on location." How analogous to the pre-call planning and on-site performing required to accomplish the successful sales call! By applying the various strategic and tactical paradigms outlined in these pages to customer needs, the salesperson first creates a mental picture of what he or she wants to happen on this specific call. With this picture in mind and without taking the spotlight off the customer's needs, the salesperson assumes a leadership role in the interaction. He or she does this by taking emotional control of the selling process.

The salesperson is always the leader in the sales situation. The customer concedes this, and is often confused and disconcerted when a salesperson doesn't assume the leadership role. After all, the customer generally comes to a sales presentation without a personal or hidden agenda. If the client takes control by default or otherwise, the salesperson will soon learn about the client's options and the competitor's advantages. The salesperson must assume this leadership role regardless of the client's community or professional status. Even when outnumbered on the client's turf, the salesperson is still the leader/director of the selling event. The sales pro knows this and acts accordingly, even if, by temperament, he or she is somewhat shy or introverted. As a result, the good salesperson takes full responsibility for the sales scenario. If he or she fails to make the sale, you will not hear scapegoating about poor sales aids or circumstances.

The real pro meticulously reviews the plan and action of the call, re-asserts self-awareness—refocuses on the customer.

A *new* beginning is born.

On the 8th of January 1972 he died. He had lived his life as a "sales" person. He had known that selling was a buying-in by the customer with heart and mind. He had sold his wares that way. Like most great salespersons, he was not afraid. He possessed social courage. He laughed and cried with an openness that did not deceive or mislead. He was a great salesman but was not held hostage by material things. People were his real interest. He gave more than he took. His death left a legacy that affected those who knew him. They were better for having known him and having bought his products. The sadness of the occasion was offset by the fact that people realized someone very special had passed their way.

The sales sheet was rich in sales as "his" people filed by. One by one they expressed the "value" his "product" had brought to their lives. Yet his personal estate was hardly worth dividing amongst his heirs. What he left was true value received that transcended the sales interaction. A part of himself was in every sale he made. He understood the "soul" of selling. He embodied it. He was a role model; he was a sales hero. He was my father.

"If you, as a salesperson, are sincere, empathetic, humble, credible, kind, and tactful and can project these qualities, you can be successful beyond your wildest imaginings. These principles constitute the soul of selling."

The soul of selling is born from within the inner sanctum of the salesperson. It breathes and thrives on the nourishment of the feeling skills: sincerity, empathy, humility, credibility, kindness, and tact. It clothes itself with the apparel of emotion. It gives more than it takes. It seeks the good. It knows that the customer must be the primary beneficiary of the selling process. It cares what happens to the customer. It combines the nuances of the human personality with functional knowledge and developed skills. It orchestrates fact, skill, and feeling with masterful strokes. It plays the symphony of winners . . . salesperson, customer, and company, winners all. It avoids devious manipulation for short-term gain. It does not harm. It does not destroy . . . it builds. It is a good soul.